I AM THE BEGINNING AND THE END

BY THE SAME AUTHOR

The Pilgrim God: A Biblical Journey
(Washington: The Pastoral Press, 1985/ Dublin: Veritas, 1990)

The Way of the Lord: A New Testament Pilgrimage
(The Pastoral Press/Veritas, 1990)

Praying the Our Father Today
(The Pastoral Press, 1992)

God of the Unexpected
(London: Geoffrey Chapman/Mowbray, 1995)

The Adventure of Holiness:
Biblical Foundations and Present-Day Perspectives
(New York: ST PAULS/Alba House, 1999)

At the Wellspring: Jesus and the Samaritan Woman
(New York: ST PAULS/Alba House, 2001)

Reading the Ten Commandments Anew:Towards a Land of Freedom
(New York: ST PAULS/Alba House, 2004)

Visit our web site at
www.albahouse.org
(for orders www.stpauls.us)

or call 1-800-343-2522 (ALBA)
and request current catalog

Brother John of Taizé

I Am the Beginning and the End

Creation Stories and Visions
of Fulfillment in the Bible

ST PAULS

Published in French by Ateliers et Presses de Taizé, 2007
under the title *Je suis le Commencement et la Fin: Récits bibliques de création et
visions de l'accomplissement.*

Library of Congress Cataloging-in-Publication Data

John de Taizé, frère.
 [Je suis le commencement et la fin. English]
 I am the beginning and the end : creation stories and visions of fulfillment in the
Bible / Brother John of Taizé.
  p. cm.
 ISBN-13: 978-0-8189-1248-1
 ISBN-10: 0-8189-1248-0
 1. Bible. O.T. Genesis I-IV—Criticism, interpretation, etc. 2. Creation—Biblical teach-
ing. 3. Bible. N.T. Revelation XVII-XXII—Criticism, interpretation, etc.
4. End of the world—Biblical teaching. I. Title.

BS1235.52.E45   2007
222'.1106—dc22

2007001923

Produced and designed in the United States of America by the
Fathers and Brothers of the Society of St. Paul,
2187 Victory Boulevard, Staten Island, New York 10314-6603
as part of their communications apostolate.

ISBN-13: 978-0-8189-1248-1
ISBN-10: 0-8189-1248-0

Printing Information:

Current Printing - first digit   1   2   3   4   5   6   7   8   9   10

Year of Current Printing - first year shown

2007   2008   2009   2010   2011   2012   2013   2014   2015   2016

Contents

Introduction

I am the Alpha and the Omega, the First and the Last,
the Beginning and the End.   (Revelation 22:13)

Who has not wondered, at one time or another, about the beginning and the end of the universe or of human history? Yet it
is not always clear to us that, in asking these questions, we leave
behind the realm of empirical observation and approach what
contemporary physicists call "singularities." By their very nature,
these unique events are outside the categories we normally use
to make sense of the world. For this reason they can never be
completely grasped by human understanding. It should not surprise us, then, that the Bible regards them as privileged moments
that awaken us to the reality of God, the unfathomable Mystery
that gives meaning and consistence to all that exists.

And yet, to discover the face of God in the Bible stories
which deal with the beginning and the end, we need to know
how to read those chapters. For a host of reasons, to many of
our contemporaries they remain a closed book. Unable to situate
them correctly, we are in danger of dismissing them out of hand,
regarding them as mere fables or works of science fiction. Or
else our preconceived ideas, the result of our religious training
or of the prejudices of today's world, form a screen between us
and the text. In this way we deprive ourselves of what in fact
are high-points of biblical revelation, a teaching which is still of

great value concerning the meaning of the universe (cosmology), of human life (anthropology) and above all of the identity of our God (theology). These fundamental questions, just as relevant today as they were thousands of years ago, receive exceptional illumination from these stories of extraordinary depth, once we have cleared away the debris that keeps us from approaching them correctly.

This book is based on Bible reflections given in Taizé as part of the international young adult meetings that take place there. It deals with the first four chapters of Genesis and the last section of the Book of Revelation. Rather than viewing these writings as an outdated alternative to scientific explanations or a film of how it was or how it will be, these pages attempt to discern in them a profound reflection on the meaning of the universe and humanity in the light of faith in God. Understood correctly, these texts break the chains of a closed world to situate our existence in the widest context possible. They allow us to discover, at the heart of all that exists, an inexhaustible Wellspring of energy and a Focus of unity, offering fulfillment in a life shared among all.

The Peaceable Kingdom

In the beginning... With a simple and apparently commonplace
Hebrew word (*bereshith*), the first chapter of the Book of Genesis
invites us at once to leave behind our ordinary way of perceiving
the world and to go where humans have no direct access. In fact,
since we are inescapably situated "in time," the only way we can
understand time is within the experience of duration, through
the contrast between the "now" of the perceiver and a "then"
that is perceived. We look back to the past through memory;
we anticipate a future in some kind of continuity with what has
already occurred. The present moment itself is a fleeting reality
impossible to grasp; as we attempt to hold on to it, it has already
eluded us. Similarly, the notion of a beginning or end to time is,
strictly speaking, unimaginable. We fall asleep every night and
we wake up every morning, but we cannot remember the precise
moment of our falling asleep and waking, because our everyday
consciousness can gain no distance on the flow of time.

In analogous fashion, to speak of a beginning of the world
is to point to what contemporary physics calls a "singularity," a
reality outside the course of time as we know it. Does it make
sense to ask what comes before the beginning? In this sense,
the beginning is not essentially chronological; it is not merely

the first item in a list. It is rather the intention that lies behind the very existence of the list itself — a qualitative shift, a "time out of time" which can only be attained by a leap of some sort, whether of faith or of reason. It should therefore come as no surprise that, in the Bible, the word *bereshith,* "in the beginning," is followed in the same sentence by the word *elohim,* "God." The two notions are intimately connected. The God of the Bible, compared to the pagan gods of old who were essentially guardians of a cosmos to which they belonged, is of another order entirely. Not located within, or subject to, our duration, God can truly be the Origin or Source of all that exists. And the first sentence of the Bible goes on to express this truth by using the verb *bara',* which we translate as "to create."

This verb, unlike the word "create" in English, does not strictly speaking refer to the act of an artist or artisan who takes what already exists and sets it in a new configuration. To create in the biblical sense means rather to bring something brand-new into being, to be the source of its existence, and in this sense it refers specifically to God, whose fundamental characteristic it is. The God of the Bible is eternal Newness and the Source of all that is new; a relationship to this God inevitably involves a participation in this Newness. In God, we are constantly being made anew.[1] Decrepitude thus implies a distancing from the Origin.

Understood in this sense, the act of creation does not simply or primarily point to a moment long ago, a chronological beginning. The notion of a chronological beginning is at best a

---

[1] For a fuller discussion of newness as an essential characteristic of God, see Brother John of Taizé, *God of the Unexpected* (London: Geoffrey Chapman/ Mowbray, 1995).

sign — one is tempted to say a sacrament — of the permanent origin of all things in God. On a deeper and truer level, creation is an ongoing relationship, an unchanging dimension of all that exists in our world. To put it another way, the God of the Bible is not rightly called the Creator because, once upon a time, in ages past, he brought things into being and then vanished back into his splendid isolation. If to speak of God as the Creator naturally entails the acknowledgment that he is the beginning and end of all that exists, it signifies even more truly the realization that all things persist in being not of their own innate power but through a relationship with Another. Nothing but God is its own Source.

This understanding of the biblical God as the eternal Source of what is new and unexpected left its mark elsewhere on the Scriptures. In the sixth century B.C.E., very possibly at about the same time as Genesis 1 was taking shape, an unnamed prophet arose in Babylon, land of exile for the ruling circles of Israel. To a people haunted by nostalgia for the great interventions of God in the past and languishing in despair at their current state, this prophet proclaimed:

> Do not recall past events;
> do not pay attention to former things.
> Look! I am doing something new.
> Now it is springing up, do you not perceive it?
> (Isaiah 43:18-19)

God, always present and always true to himself, is fully capable of repeating the miracle of the Exodus, and can even reenact the calling into being of the universe (compare Isaiah 43:19b and Genesis 2:6) to save his demoralized people. In this sense, every act of God is a "new creation," bringing a heightened level of existence, life and meaning to what otherwise would harden into immobility and meaninglessness. *He sends forth his word and the ice melts, blows his wind and the waters flow* (Psalm 147:18).

To understand the authentic import of the first chapters of the Book of Genesis, then, we need to keep in mind this specific biblical understanding of creation. A so-called fundamentalist or literal reading, which views them as a kind of film of "what really happened long ago" is in fact untrue to their basic thrust. In speaking about the beginning, a place to which they can have no direct access, the inspired authors want to tell us something essential about who God is and who we are as God's creation. They do this in the only way they can: by taking elements of the world as we know it and projecting them back in time. This is the same procedure, incidentally, followed by scientists, and indeed by anyone who seeks to describe or understand something through the use of human reason. We can only attempt to grasp the unknown by placing it in relationship with what we already know.

Indeed, the true difference between the biblical account of creation and a scientific study of the origins of the universe lies not so much in the method employed as in the questions that are asked. Whereas the physicists and evolutionary biologists of today are primarily interested in understanding the mechanisms by which the world and life as we know them came about and how they continue to function, the authors of the first chapters of the Bible were concerned rather to link the history of Israel and its God to humanity and the universe as a whole. Their primary aim was to confess their faith that, far from being a tribal deity merely anxious to further the cause of one particular people, the God who had broken into their life was truly universal, deeply involved in the existence and the fate of all that exists. In addition, the stories they told attempted to show how the world as we know it follows from the being and the existence of this God. What belongs to its fundamental characteristics as created by God, and what is instead a departure from its identity as God's creation? To understand our origins in this way is in fact to have a kind of blueprint for right living, for an existence in harmony with reality; in this respect, the concern of the biblical authors was anything but theoretical. To use a word we will have other occasions to repeat in these pages, their endeavor was part of the search for **wisdom**.

A Twofold Approach

For a long time now, Bible scholars have been in agreement that the Book of Genesis was not written by a single author from start to finish but brings together material from different sources. It seems evident that there are not one but two creation stories at the beginning of the book, later joined together to form a composite whole. Until recently, the received opinion has been that the first account (Genesis 1:1-2:4a) is in fact the more recent, belonging to the so-called Priestly school and dating from the Babylonian exile in the sixth century B.C.E. The second account (Genesis 2:4b-3:24) was dated as far back as the time of Solomon and attributed to the so-called Yahwist source. Lately this hypothesis has been called into question, although no new consensus has as yet emerged among scholars. One tendency today is to see the second account of creation as later than the first, possibly post-exilic in origin.

Obviously, dating written material on the basis of the text

alone is an extremely hazardous business, especially if it is rooted in oral traditions that were recounted over and over again, then put into writing and perhaps rewritten more than once. Given such a process, what does the notion of dating even mean? Are we not in a situation analogous to what was said above regarding the impossibility of fixing an absolute beginning to time? Stories and texts have a life of their own; they grow and evolve in the course of the ages. Perhaps the principal advantage of contemporary research is to help us realize that the history of a text is far more complex than we may have imagined.

In any case, if we compare the style of the two accounts of creation, we notice a manifest difference. The second account is a narrative, with a naïve feel to it that reminds us of the stories we heard or read as children — a man and woman in a garden, a talking snake, a deity who plays with dirt and takes walks in the evening to enjoy a cool breeze.... Whether this archaic style is original or simulated (and there is some reason to think that the final version of the story is the product of sophisticated circles, which does not, however, necessarily imply an exilic or post-exilic dating), it clearly distinguishes chapters 2 and 3 from the first chapter, which is not in fact a "story" at all, insofar as it has no dramatic interest. It is closer in form to a poem or a song, since it is crafted out of different kinds of rhythms, both of form and content. It is also more "scientific" and therefore more modern in tone than the second account. There is no personification of non-human realities, but rather a deep interest in classification that betrays keen powers of empirical observation: plants and animals are carefully distinguished on the basis of criteria such as habitat and the kinds of seeds produced. Though this first account of creation describes the origin of the universe not along the lines of our contemporary scientific understanding but according to the worldview current at the time, there is very little that is mythological about it. God remains a ubiquitous presence, but always in the background, so to speak. The divine transcendence is safeguarded (no walking in the garden here!) and the coming into being of the universe follows a logic which is predominately immanent, in other words conditioned by the object itself — the world that gradually takes shape before the reader's eyes.

It is instructive to compare Genesis 1 with contemporaneous accounts of creation current in the civilizations that surrounded Israel. In these stories, the universe generally comes into being through some kind of warfare with the forces of chaos or evil. In Babylon we find the tale of Marduk, who becomes the supreme deity by defeating Tiamat, a sea-monster, and fashioning the universe from her body. Such myths have also left their mark on the Hebrew Scriptures, though only as vestiges. Psalm 89, for example, offers us in passing an allusion to creation in which the God of Israel plays a role akin to that of Marduk, while Tiamat becomes Rahab (or in other texts, Leviathan):

> Lord God of hosts, who is like you?
> Mighty Lord, your steadfastness surrounds you.
> You dominate the raging of the sea;
> when the waves swell, you quiet them.
> You crushed Rahab and stabbed him to death;
> with your powerful arm you scattered your enemies.
> Yours is the sky and yours the earth;
> you set the world and everything in it
> on firm foundations....
> (Psalm 89:9-11; cf. Job 26:12-13; Isaiah 27:1)

Elsewhere, the victory over chaos at the creation of the universe is merged with the crossing of the Red Sea following the liberation from Egypt:

> Arise, arise,
> put on strength, arm of the Lord!
> Arise as in days of old,
> generations long ago.
> Was it not you who cut Rahab into pieces,
> stabbed the sea-monster?
> Was it not you who dried up the sea,
> the waters of the great deep?
> Who made the depths of the sea a road
> for those redeemed to cross?
>   (Isaiah 51:9-10; cf. Psalm 74:13-15)

The contrast between these texts and Genesis 1 is striking. In the latter passage, the element of combat in the act of creating has been reduced to the extreme. God is so utterly beyond the rest of what exists that there is no need for a bitter struggle with any countervailing forces. Unlike so many other creation stories, the text thus exudes a serenity that is truly impressive. The world is born under the sign of peace, as a kind of untroubled blossoming of the Creator's intention. Rather than being rooted in images of warfare and conflict, the creative act is likened instead to an artistic endeavor, a symbolic act. If sea-monsters are mentioned (Genesis 1:21), they are only considered as one of the many beings created by God; this detail may well be intentional, as in other later texts where even the sea-monsters are summoned to praise God (Psalm 148:7) or where Leviathan's creation is attributed to the divine sense of humor (Psalm 104:26).

It is nonetheless true that Genesis 1 does not escape entirely the notion of a struggle against something that resists. To put it another way, the possibility of a true *creatio ex nihilo* is not yet thinkable.[2] Like a human artist, in both accounts of creation in Genesis God operates upon raw materials. In chapter 1, before the creative Word there is the *tohu wabohu,* the primordial chaos, the dark waters. Here the theme of the archaic dragon or sea-monster appears in significantly attenuated form. There is also present a *ruach elohim,* interpreted by some as a "powerful wind" that is another expression of chaos, but understood by the major representatives of the Judeo-Christian tradition as "the Spirit of God" hovering over the waters to subdue them. This reading is supported by the verb, which is found only one other time in the Pentateuch, namely in Deuteronomy 32:11, where it is applied to God described as an eagle watching over her young. According to this interpretation, God creates by means of his breath and his word working in tandem (cf. Psalm 33:6). The early Christians naturally understood this as a foreshadowing of the doctrine of the Trinity.[3] In any case, in the early chapters of our Bible God is not described as a victorious warrior, but as a transcendent source of harmony and peace.

---

[2] "Nothingness" conceived (paradoxically) as a positive notion, as something thinkable, only arrived on the scene at a surprisingly late hour. In strictly mathematical terms, this is shown by the discovery of zero. See Charles Seife, *Zero: The Biography of a Dangerous Idea* (New York: Penguin Books, 2000).

[3] St. Irenaeus, bishop of Lyons in the second century, speaks of the Word (made flesh in Jesus Christ) and the Spirit as the "two hands of God" working together to create the universe and especially the human race. See his work *Adversus Haereses* I,22,1; IV, Pr.,4; 7,4; V,1,3; 5,1; 6,1; 28,4.

The Rhythms of Creation

In Genesis 1, the act of creation consists essentially in establishing a certain order in what was heretofore chaos. For many of our contemporaries, the word "order" carries negative or at least misleading connotations, exactly like another biblical word that has often been coupled with it, namely "law." Both words suggest to many people in the Western world today an oppressive and arbitrary power that seeks to thwart the spontaneous movement of life. This is perhaps not surprising, because history is full of attempts by one part of humankind, the more powerful and privileged part, to impose its notion of "the way things should be" on the rest of our race, and even on the material universe, as the ecological movement has never tired of pointing out. In the face of such attempts, freedom necessarily involves liberating oneself from an unjust order, and indeed the second book of the Bible, the foundational narrative of God's people Israel, tells such a story, that of a group of slaves who found new life by being liberated by a "pilgrim God" and brought to a land of freedom. Is Genesis 1 therefore a step backward? Is the God who brings order out of chaos merely a more powerful version of Pharaoh, king of Egypt?

In fact, as the Exodus story demonstrates well if we read it attentively, liberation from an unjust order, however necessary, is not the sufficient cause of true freedom. In one way or another, human beings need to organize their lives. Existence is not merely the random play of atoms, or no one would be around to tell the story. If the biblical God is the one who liberates from slavery, that God is also the one who offers a new way for humans to live together, in a society founded not on oppression but on solidarity and harmony. Consenting to follow the pilgrim God towards the land of promise means trusting in that God and drawing the appropriate conclusions for life together with others. Expressed in more biblical terms, the covenant with God involves of necessity the commandments, a coherent vision of how to structure human life that follows from the identity of that God. If the Egyptian Pharaoh, the divinities of Mesopotamia and the Baals of Canaan had their definition of world order and their means for achieving it, their *sedeq* and *mishpat* (words usually translated by "justice/righteousness" and "judgment"), so of necessity did the God of Israel. The question then is not whether order is necessary, but what order corresponds to the true functioning of the universe and thus makes authentic fulfillment for its inhabitants possible, allowing them to become what in reality they are.

The first account of creation in Genesis, then, describes the coming into being of all that exists as the establishment of God's order or justice. Perhaps we would be closer to the mark if we substituted for the term "order" the expression "the rhythms (or melodies) of creation." This would help us to realize that we are not talking about some static or immobile framework imposed from without, which does violence to the natural dynamism of existence, but rather of regularities which foster growth, harmony and beauty. It is something analogous to the kind of order that turns random sounds into Mozart's clarinet concerto, the revelation of a transcendent meaning which, far from negating what exists, places it in a context that reveals vistas of significance beyond anything that could previously have been imagined.[4]

---

[4] For a beautiful and suggestive description of creation through music, in a fictional universe, see the cosmology of J.R.R. Tolkien, *The Silmarillion* (New York: Ballantine Books, 2002), especially the first work, *Ainulindalë*, or "The Music of the Ainur."

To name this order which I have described as rhythm, we could also use the Greek word *logos*. While often translated as "word" in our Bibles, *logos* can also refer to the underlying "logic" or meaning of a reality. God's creative word, the divine Logos, thus becomes immanent in creation and gives it its intrinsic significance, its deepest logic. We are not far here from the insight of Saint John in the prologue to his Gospel when he writes, *In the beginning was the Logos... All things were made through him* (John 1:1, 3). Here, John simply thematizes and brings into relationship with Jesus Christ what Genesis 1 already shows after its own fashion. God creates, not through some titanic combat with the forces of evil but by speaking, by sending forth a word (cf. Psalm 147:15). That word determines the essential lineaments of all that exists and makes of it a language that reveals the identity of the living God.

Days and Words

If Genesis 1 describes the act of creation as essentially one of establishing order, rhythm or structure, then it follows that the structure of the text itself is particularly important since, just as in the case of music, form is also content. One structure revealed even by a cursory reading has to do with time — the seven days of the week. Right from the start, then, we see that the passage of time is of great import to the biblical author. The text presents a progressive coming into being of the universe in chronological stages, so that our modern theories of evolution, however different they may be in their details and in their underlying motivation, are not as alien to the biblical account as is sometimes assumed.

Creation is thus described as a primordial week. Upon closer examination, however, it becomes evident that this week is unlike any other, since the sun, which in our world determines the existence and length of a day, does not appear until the fourth "day" of creation. So why this structure?

First of all, unlike the day, the month and the year, a week is not based upon the regularities of nature; from a purely natural perspective it is arbitrary. The traditional Roman week, for example, had eight days. The seven-day week only took hold in Rome after Constantine's conversion to Christianity. Why seven days? The reason remains shrouded in mystery, but based on the names of the days in many civilizations, a possible explanation is astrological: there were seven known planets (including the sun and the moon). The biblical week, however, does not follow this logic, but is simply structured around the Sabbath. When we realize that Genesis 1 may well have been set down in writing by priests of Israel exiled in Babylon, and that astrology played an important role in the Babylonian religion, we are tempted to discern a polemical motivation here, at least in part, in other words the use of contrast so as better to show the specific nature of the revelation to Israel. The week did not come into being, the text seems to say, because of the heavenly bodies, considered as preexistent divine beings. Rather, God first created the week and then set within it the stars and planets. The week exists because it is the basic framework of God's creative act.

To put it another way, although the inspired author may have organized the creation narrative around the week because it was one of the fundamental means of structuring time available to him, by so doing that author says in fact that every week is a representation, literally a "making present," of God's creative act. Every Monday, every Tuesday, and so forth comes directly from the hand of God. The week is a kind of sacrament or efficacious sign that recalls and makes present the Creator God. It reveals to us the essence of time — an alternation or rhythm that moves towards the Day of the Lord. In and through the passing of time, something is revealed that does not pass: the creative presence of God that gives existence and meaning to all that exists. Once again, the concern of the biblical author is to convince us that creation is not just something relegated to a long-ago past; each week makes the Origin present — not chronologically, but symbolically.

Although the most obvious structure of Genesis 1 is provided by the week of days, there is in addition a more hidden rhythm in the text. We have seen that here God creates by speaking, and so another regularity comes from the repetition of the expression *"And God said...."* If we count the number of times this expression is used, we do not come up with the number seven, as we might expect, but rather ten. Creation comes about through ten words or utterances from God. This is significant, because the expression "the Ten Words" refers first of all to what Christians call "the ten commandments" and which form the nucleus of the Torah (Exodus 20:1-17; Deuteronomy 5:6-21), God's revelation to Israel that created a covenant and made them into his people.[5] We are thus invited to superpose Genesis 1 upon the story of Israel and to understand each in terms of the other. The Bible tells us in effect that the same divine Word which is the origin of all that exists was revealed to Israel as the source of its own existence as God's people (cf. Psalm 147:15-20). God

---

[5]   See Brother John of Taizé, *Reading the Ten Commandments Anew: Towards a Land of Freedom* (New York: ST PAULS/Alba House, 2004).

both *calls what is not into being* (Romans 4:17) and calls human beings to become a *holy nation*, a sign of his presence in the world, by *keeping his covenant* (Exodus 19:5-6), recapitulated in the Ten Words. What appears as two separate events on the side of human beings is one and the same for God. Although its effects are different according to the situation, God's Word is always equal to itself, always life-giving, always calling into being what is new.

World as Language

On the first day, and with the first word, God calls light into existence. Here we have another surprisingly modern feature of this text, since contemporary accounts of the origin of the universe start with an explosion of energy, the so-called Big Bang, whereas the stars only come into being in function of this. Can we discern again a polemical intention in Genesis, the concern to deny any divine character to the heavenly bodies? In any case, the priority of light recalls to us a characteristic of the manifestation of the divine in the ancient world. In the so-called theophanies or appearances of God, light is always a prominent feature. If the God of the Bible, *wrapped in light as in a cloak* (Psalm 104:2), has a particular affinity with light, that says something about the divine identity. The New Testament goes a step further: *God is light, and in him there is no darkness at all* (1 John 1:5). Light is radiating energy, diffusing further and further outward of its own essence, constantly communicating itself until some extraneous reality blocks its path. It thus shows God to be primordial generosity. As the philosophers of old put it: the good tends to diffuse itself (*bonum diffusum sui*). Light is also beautiful, and allows everything else to be revealed as beautiful: *In your light we see the light* (Psalm 36:9). The universe is not ethically or aesthetically neutral — it is the good and beautiful creation of a God who is the Source of all good and Prototype of all beauty.

The structure of the first day provides important clues as to how the inspired author conceived the creative act of God.

> And God said "Let there be light" and there was light.
> And God saw that the light was good.
> And God separated the light and the darkness.
> And God called the light "day" and the darkness "night."
> And there was evening and there was morning: first day.
>
> (Genesis 1:3-5)

First of all, God calls the light into being by means of his word alone, with no struggle, violence or even effort apparently required. It would not be too much to say, in fact, that the light is in some sense identical with the word that speaks it; it is a symbolic communication of the divine being. Then, God verifies that the light is good, in harmony with his being, and separates it from the darkness. We might expect that, if God is all-powerful and if the light, good and beautiful, corresponds to his identity, then the light would simply take over and cause the darkness to vanish forever. This, however, would not correspond to the universe as we know it. Although the darkness is not said to be good or created by God, it is not merely annihilated by the light. It is "saved" or "redeemed" by being set in a broader context. From the very start, then, one of the components of the creative act is salvation.

In fact, the process of creation in Genesis 1 is more complex than a mere bringing into being. It involves a separation that does not lead to destruction but to a different kind of unity. After the light is separated from the darkness, it is reunited to it in a new way. We now have two heretofore inexistent realities, "day" and "night," which join together to form the first day. The act of naming, incidentally, is a typically biblical expression to indicate the creation of something new: to be named is to have one's identity formally recognized and ratified, to be "called into being" in the strongest sense of that expression.

God's creative work in Genesis 1 has been termed "creation by separation."[6] One could also use the term "differentiation." The creation of the universe involves passing from an undifferentiated whole (the *tohu wabohu* of 1:2) through separation to the existence of a new kind of structured whole formed by the union of the different parts. Division or separation is required not as an end in itself, but as a necessary prelude to union. In this union, the character of each element is safeguarded, but it finds its meaning as part of a wider context. Unity is not fusion, but preserves diversity within itself. Here again we come up against the biblical notion of order as dynamic structure, a kind of cosmic dance or symphony.

Right at the beginning of the Bible, this passage thus witnesses to the primordial importance of **relationship** in the Judeo-Christian tradition. And relationship involves by its very nature the notion of **difference**. In this tradition, then, differences are not seen as negative in themselves, as evidence of an imperfection needing to be healed or overcome. The ideal

---

6 The late French biblical scholar Paul Beauchamp was the one who brought to light this aspect of creation, most thoroughly in his work *Création et separation. Étude exégétique du chapitre premier de la Genèse* (Paris: Bibliothèque des Sciences religieuses, 1969).

state of being is not a homogenous, undifferentiated whole, but rather a chorus of different voices that sing in harmony. Peace is thus possible through respect for diversity; a totalitarian violence which would abolish all variety in the name of unity is not the fundamental law of the universe.[7]

It is significant that Genesis 1 is generally considered to be the work of priests at the time of the Babylonian exile. Those whose task it is to codify and interpret the law are particularly apt to understand the importance of distinctions. Their work is precisely that of discovering and applying the appropriate distinctions. Contemporary society, for its part, does not in general have a healthy outlook on the law. Today in the West we tend to veer from an unreflective libertarianism or antinomianism, whereby all law or distinction is seen as a form of violence, to an authoritarian mindset that ultimately seeks to repress all spontaneity and novelty in the name of abstract norms. Both attitudes are in fact expressions of the same basic misunderstanding, which Genesis 1 in its own way attempts to remedy. Creation is neither the exacerbation of chaos nor its abolition, but the establishment of correct differences and distances which bring a dynamic structure into being, a work of beauty in which the relationships between the elements become bearers of meaning. It would not be too far-fetched to say that the act of creation is essentially the origin of language, or more exactly of the universe as God's language.

---

[7] The contrast between the Bible's "rhetoric of peace" and the "grammar of violence" that marks both the pagan and post-modern worldviews has been worked out magisterially by David Bentley Hart in his book *The Beauty of the Infinite: The Aesthetics of Christian Truth* (Grand Rapids: Eerdmans, 2003).

Setting the Stage

The progressive coming into being of the universe in the first six days of creation follows a very logical development. It is akin to what one would do if one wished to put on a play. The theater and the stage are first built, and then peopled with characters. Similarly, in the course of the first half of the week, the stage of the world is set. And this again takes place through separations. For the earth to appear, the waters have to be divided. And so the sky is created. For the ancients the sky is not merely a vast space that contains the heavenly bodies, as modern science tells us, but is constituted by a kind of dividing-wall, hard and perhaps transparent, that holds back the waters above and opens up a space for further developments. This wall or firmament, seen from the other side, is a kind of *pavement of blue stone, as translucent as the sky itself* (Exodus 24:10b), and it reappears in the last book of the Bible as *a sea transparent as crystal* (Revelation 4:6).

Next, a similar separation takes place in the waters below, so that dry land can appear. We should note in passing that the Israelites were never a seafaring folk. Dry land for them was a bulwark of security; the sea a place of peril. This outlook finds an echo in those ancient myths of creation as a struggle with the sea-monster, but as in Genesis 1, it can also be expressed in a more rational form. In Psalm 104, by his word God commands the waters to leave the land and retire to the place assigned to them:

> At your rebuke, [the waters] take flight;
> at the sound of your thunder, they run away in alarm.
> They climb the mountains; they descend the valleys
> to the place you assigned for them.

> You set a boundary not to be crossed
> so they do not turn back and cover the earth again.
>   (Psalm 104:7-9; cf. Jeremiah 5:22)

Once the dry land exists, it is covered with carpeting and
scenery, with vegetation. Here, separation takes the form of
distinction. Different kinds of plants are carefully distinguished
from one another, in all likelihood according to the mode of
reproduction — the grasses with no visible seed, the grains with
their seeds on top, and the trees with seed hidden in their fruits.
This betrays careful observation and a love of classification. Once
again, a too-facile differentiation between religion and science
can mislead us. In this text, a rudimentary scientific outlook is
quite evident.

After the stage has been built and the scenery set up, the
electrician is called in to take care of the lights. In any structure based on the number seven, the number four stands at the
center. We can therefore confidently expect that the fourth day,
coinciding with the fifth word, will be of particular importance. It
marks the climax of the first period of creation, and the prelude
to the second. We might well wonder, though, why the creation
of the heavenly bodies is placed at such a key juncture.

It has often been remarked that in this passage the sun and
the moon are not named, but referred to as *the big lamp* and *the
little lamp*. Here we have another example of the "modernity" of
this text (perhaps again with a polemical intent). Unlike what we
find in the religion of Mesopotamia, the sun, moon and stars are
not supernatural beings. Nor, it should be emphasized, are they
merely passive objects. They are intermediate beings created by
God to play a particular role in the life of the world. And their
function is not primarily, as we might expect, to give light to the
earth. That is only mentioned as an afterthought. The first role

of the heavenly bodies is to **separate** *day and night... light and darkness* (Genesis 1:14, 18) and to be *signs* that mark days and years. If creation, for the author of Genesis 1, is essentially the establishment of a dynamic order, a structure that gives regularity to movement, then it is clear that this act is recapitulated in the work of the fourth day, which explains why it forms the center of the text. For the priests of Israel, the creation of the heavenly bodies is equivalent to the institution of the calendar, whereby time is organized in function of the people's relationship with God by means of recurring feasts and seasons. The calendar is thus not a human invention; God is the one who has set these regularities in the very fabric of reality. Here we are not far from what a later age will refer to as the "laws of nature." If the stars are said to *govern* day and night (Genesis 1:18), this is not by determining behavior along the lines of the pagan gods (Israel's faith remained implacably opposed to astrology), but because of their quality as signs; they are like traffic signals. The God of the Bible governs the world by means of his word, and one way this word is manifested is by the symbols he has placed in the heavens.

Now that the stage has been set, the characters can be introduced. The fifth day sees the appearance of the animals that fill sea and air, each *according to its species* (Genesis 1:21). The passage from inanimate to animate creatures is marked in this passage by the notion of **blessing**. The prerogative of God, to bless, means to bestow a greater measure of life. Here, it describes the gift of life itself. Elsewhere, it is employed to refer to all that makes life full and worth living — a homeland, children, food and clothing, etc. God's blessing is a supremely dynamic reality, bequeathing to creatures a share in the divine creative power. God will not have to create from nothing, by an independent act, each generation of living beings. The created universe acquires more and more self-determination through its relationship with the Source.

On the sixth day two creative words are spoken. The first applies to the animals that fill the earth, again divided into three classes — domestic animals, wild animals, and *those that creep* (Genesis 1:24-25). Surprisingly, these creatures are not given a blessing; the blessing on the land will be reserved for human beings, to which the animals are subordinate. For now, at the end of the sixth day, the main character of the drama is finally introduced, the protagonist of the story. Simply by placing the creation of human beings here, at the end of this long development, the text shows the key and indeed unique position of human beings in the world created by God.

Created in God's Image

In addition to placing it at the end of this long series, the narrative shows the importance of this new creative act by a change in syntax. Until now God always used a form of the verb customarily employed to express wishes or commands: *Let there be... Let the earth produce....* Now the verb shifts to the plural: *Let us make....* Although the form may come from the archaic notion of the heavenly court, with God in the role of a king speaking to his counselors, what it in fact suggests in the text as we have it is a reflective pause in the divine activity. God steps back and enters into himself, so to speak, before taking this new step. This implies that the result of this word will be a being more intimately related to the Creator, arising from a deeper and more inward participation in the divine life than that enjoyed by the rest of the created universe. The following words will make more explicit what this special status entails.

What is created at the end of the sixth day is *adam*, which unfortunately, as a result of the following chapters, has taken on the quality of a proper name. In fact it is a collective noun, rendered best in English by the now old-fashioned and politically incorrect "man," and today by "humanity" or "humankind." Here it does not refer to one being, or even to one couple, but rather to the human race as distinguished from the various species of plants and animals.

Alone among the creatures, *adam* is defined as *in [God's] image, as [God's] likeness* (Genesis 1:26), and the word "image" is repeated again twice in the following verse to define the special relationship between the Creator and human beings. In the course of thousands of years, much reflection has gone into trying to determine exactly what gives humankind this status. A full investigation of this topic would take us beyond the bounds of our study and would require a book of its own. But before we examine what information the text itself provides concerning the question, it is helpful to grasp a more fundamental and often overlooked point which arises from the biblical context itself. It has already been noted that this account of creation seems to have been elaborated, or at least given its final form, in dialogue with other creation stories and other cultures, a dialogue which most often took the form of an implicit contrast or opposition. If the Book of Genesis was indeed edited by priests during or immediately after the Babylonian exile in the sixth century before our era, then one would expect that the religion of that powerful nation would have an impact on the formulation of Israel's foundational narratives. And one of the constant criticisms of the pagan religions by the Jews was that these religions depicted their deities in visible form — statues of birds, animals or even human beings. As opposed to these inner-worldly gods, *the work of human hands*, the God of Israel is beyond all things and at the same time is the Source of all that exists (cf. Psalm 115:3-4).

In other words, while the surrounding nations make gods in the image of visible and this-worldly realities, the invisible God of Israel creates human beings in the divine image! This implicit contrast may well be the most salient feature of the biblical affirmation that humanity is created in the image of God. It implies moreover that human beings are not like God because of something visible in them, but rather that their visibility enables the God who is beyond all visible images to be present in the world through beings who can be perceived. Again, we are in a universe whose logic can be called symbolic, or better, sacramental. *Adam* is the tangible sign of an intangible reality. Here we already have in embryo the basic understanding of the world which will make it possible, centuries later, for Christian theologians to speak of God becoming incarnate in his Son, Jesus the Messiah.

And there is, in fact, an intimate link between the notion of "image" and that of "son." In chapter 5 of the Book of Genesis, we read:

> When Adam had lived 130 years, he fathered a child in his likeness, according to his image, and gave him the name Seth.   (Genesis 5:3)

The son is in the image of his father, and thus the divine image continues to inform the whole human race.

Let us take a step further, now, and ask ourselves what features of humanity render it capable of bearing and communicating the divine image. The first thing the text tells us is that humans are invited by God to have dominion over all the other living creatures of sea, air and land. The verb *radah* can indeed have the negative connotation expressed by our verb "to dominate," and this fact has sometimes been used to justify criticisms of the Judeo-Christian tradition as responsible for the pillaging and pollution of nature characteristic of modern Western civilization. The same verb, however, can be used in a more neutral way, simply to describe the role of a ruler, and this would appear to be more consonant with the tone of this chapter where, as we have seen, all violence is carefully excluded from the divine image. By describing humanity as being in the divine image and consequently as ruling over the other creatures, the text does not wish to describe *adam* as a bully, but merely to say that he is the regent or viceroy of the invisible God.

Moreover, to understand correctly the role of a king in the Bible, we must not take a tyrant or a corrupt ruler as our model, but rather the **ideal** of kingship as it is portrayed in the sacred texts, even if there is an inevitable gap between this ideal and the reality on the ground. Basically, the role of a king is to ensure harmony and justice in society, and therefore to stand up for those who have no one to take their side. This is evident in the portrait of the ideal king given in Psalm 72:

> In his days justice will flourish
> and great peace until the moons end.
> He will have dominion from sea to sea
> from the River to the ends of the earth.
> For he will rescue the needy who cry for help
> and the poor who have no one to help them.
> He will look with compassion on the powerless
> and the needy
> and save the life of the poor.   (Psalm 72:7-8, 12-13)

This king's power is only experienced as subjugation by whatever threatens life (*Before him the wild beast will bend his knee*, v. 9). This may explain the verb used in Genesis 1:28, where humankind is enjoined to "subdue" (*kabash*) the earth. There is perhaps a reminiscence here of the older idea of a struggle against the forces of chaos, but in the final version of the text this is significantly attenuated. If God exercises dominion in this chapter primarily through the efficacious power of his word, then it is reasonable to assume that human beings, as God's regents, are called to fulfill their mission to create harmony in the universe in a similar non-violent fashion. As the reflective, thinking part of creation, they receive the vocation to use their wisdom to maintain and preserve the natural order established by God. The modern ecological sensibility need not look solely for extra-biblical sources to justify and explain its concerns; a responsible stewardship of the earth follows directly from the biblical understanding of humanity's place in the created order.

Unity in Diversity

Human beings are thus in God's image, first of all, when they use their intelligence to create peace and harmony on earth. The following verse shows another aspect of their unique identity:

> God created humankind in his image,
> in the image of God he created him,
> male and female he created them.   (Genesis 1:27)

Once again, God creates by means of separation. Since we have already examined the significance of creation by separation in Genesis 1, we are well equipped to understand the meaning of this verse. Human beings are not divided into two independent groups, the "males" and the "females," which have nothing to do with one another, like followers of different religions each worshipping in their own temples, or which constantly compete, like members of two rival sports teams. Just as day and night join together to form one day, each taking its meaning from the relationship with the other, so too humanity is created to live in relationship, for mutual belonging. Diversity is at the service of unity.

This verse shows well in what the oneness of humankind consists. It is not that of a monolithic bloc, of the reproduction of a uniform model, but rather that of a differentiated whole. Each individual, created as male or female, is incomplete, needing others to live fully his or her calling. The fact that we are sexual beings means first of all that we are not self-contained but made for relationship, for community. In this sense, the male-female polarity points beyond itself and stands for all the differences among human beings. It expresses in biological terms a basic ontological truth of the human condition. In God's creative project, diversity is not an excuse for withdrawal into a closed circle of those like me or a problem that needs to be solved through assimilation or conquest, but rather the necessary prerequisite for union. It follows that human beings are in God's image and likeness when they accept others as other without trying to make them over into their own image. They are in God's image when they respect differences and consider them as part of a wider and deeper unity rooted in God.

After creating human beings as male and female, God blesses them. This blessing enables them to multiply without endangering their unity and thus to exercise their vocation of ruling over the other creatures. It can be seen as a special mark of God's assistance to beings that otherwise would not stand out from the rest of the animal kingdom.

The tenth and final creative word in the chapter deals with food. God gives humans and animals all the plants to eat. In God's original creative intention, then, human beings are vegetarians! Violence even against animals is implicitly proscribed. Here we have another sign, if one were needed, that human beings are called to rule in the image of God through non-violent means, through the power of the word. God's final creative touch is to ratify the earth as a peaceable kingdom.

The inspired authors who set down this vision of the universe were certainly aware that it was in some sense a utopia, not identical with the empirical world as they knew it. The biblical account of history tells how, from the start, human beings did not correspond fully to the divine call, and this causes God to regret his original choice and to decide to make a new beginning (Genesis 6:5-7). This becomes explicit in the story of the great Flood, a powerful example of "de-creation" by which the waters come back and the universe returns momentarily to its original chaotic state. When things begin again, there is a new blessing (Genesis 9:1-7), but this time with a significant difference. In the new order established by God, humans are explicitly given the right to slaughter animals for food. They must not, however, eat the blood of the animals, which represents their life and belongs exclusively to God. Nor are they permitted to shed human blood, and this prohibition is now given another justification: humans are in the image of God.[8]

---

[8] See Paul Beauchamp, "Création et fondation de la loi en Genesis 1,1 - 2,4," in *La Création dans l'Orient ancien*, Lectio divina, 127 (Paris: Cerf, 1987), pp. 139-182; *Ibid.*, "La violence dans la Bible," in *Testament biblique* (Paris: Bayard, 2001), esp. pp. 169-176.

Here we are in the presence of a very reflective and profound theology. Although all violence is distasteful to God and is not part of his original conception, God now tolerates a minimum of violence as a concession to human weakness. But God nonetheless places reminders in the created order of his original intent. For Israel, the prohibition against consuming blood serves as a reminder that all life belongs to God and remains under the divine protection. It tells believers furthermore that the world as it is currently configured is the fruit of compromise and is not the definitive reality. A space is thus opened up for hope, the conviction that things need not always be the way they are now. In the writings of the great prophets of Israel, for example, the vision of a peaceable kingdom kept this hope alive amidst all the degradations of the present:

Wolves will dwell with lambs
and leopards lie down with kids.
Calves and young lions will feed together;
a little child will herd them.
Cows and bears will graze together;
their offspring will rest on the same spot.
Lions will eat straw like cows.
Infants will play on the cobra's den
and babies reach out their hands on the serpent's lair.
No harm, no ruin
on all my holy mountain,
for the land will be filled with knowledge of the Lord
as the waters fill the sea.   (Isaiah 11:6-9)

In its own way, Genesis 1 witnesses to the same dialectic. Although the world as we know it has many flaws, God is not responsible for them, and therefore it is not illusory to long for a world that is truly in the divine image, a world of justice and peace. Reality as seen by God is closer to the deepest aspirations of human beings for good than it is to the empirical situation of history blemished by rivalry and greed.

An Extra Day?

In six days, then, the universe is brought into being and qualified as *very good*, coming from God's hands as a finished product (Genesis 1:31-2:1). The narrative could logically have ended there, and this is what Genesis 2:1 seems to indicate; the verse acts as a kind of grand finale and offers the image of a closed and perfect totality:

> And so the heavens and the earth were completed and all their array.   (Genesis 2:1)

This conclusion is premature, however, since the biblical week has not six but seven days. So the first account of creation goes on to a seventh day, the Sabbath, which could seem like an afterthought that disturbs the harmony but which in fact holds the key to understanding the entire week and therefore the deepest meaning of all that exists.

Looked at from the point of view of the human logic of production and efficiency, the seventh day is indeed useless. God does nothing; he *stops* or *rests*. The closed totality represented by the six days is thus broken open by the addition of an apparently empty space. And it is this open space that keeps the week, and therefore the universe, from remaining closed up within itself in self-sufficient complacency. In this sense, the seventh day is the signature of God on the work of creation, and so it is appropriate that this day be blessed and made holy by God (Genesis 2:3). God places a wellspring of life within time, a pointer to another more fundamental dimension, the promise of a new beginning. In celebrating the weekly Sabbath, the heart of the Ten Words (see Exodus 20:8-11), Israel constantly remembers that the deepest meaning of the universe lies not within it but in its relationship to the Source.

God endowed the world with a certain autonomy, and this is well expressed by the first six days of creation taken as a whole. This autonomy is a mark of God's esteem and respect for the work of his hands. God does not wish to treat his creation as a purely passive reality, as a mother does her newborn child. Just as good parents give their children the tools to live their own lives, God intends the world, and especially human beings, to run to a great extent on its own. We may sometimes wish that God would be more visibly present, showing us the way forward, and it happens that we interpret his apparent absence as a lack of concern. But to continue with our parental metaphor, good parents must know when to step back and "hide" so that their offspring can grow and discover for themselves how to live. In that case, their discretion is in fact a sign of their trust. More often than we realize, perhaps, God's silence is likewise a sign of his trust in us.

This autonomy, however, remains relative. And here we encounter again the mystery of the seventh day. When human beings forget that they are not the Source, they close off themselves and their world and lose the secret of its fruitfulness. No longer in touch with the spring of living water, humans are forced to drink from cracked cisterns that hold no water (cf. Jeremiah 2:13), running here and there in a frenetic search to satisfy their thirst. The six days made into an absolute become a prison[9] that places its inmates before an impossible alternative: either resign oneself to spurious satisfactions or search vainly for a way out. The "extra day" of the Sabbath, then, turns out to be the hidden cornerstone that allows the entire edifice to remain standing. It safeguards the autonomy of the created order while rooting it in another dimension, from which it receives sustenance and meaning. Like God, we too are invited to stop periodically and contemplate the universe, discovering in it the fingerprints of its maker.

Questions for Reflection

1. Where do you see God doing a "new thing" in your life, in the world?
2. What changes in our life when we believe in a Creator God?
3. Do I see order as something positive or negative? What kind of order allows life to develop authentically? What kind of order stifles or inhibits true life?

---

[9] We should recall that in the Book of Revelation, the *number of the Beast*, the ruler of this world in opposition to God, is 666 (Revelation 13:18). Although many explanations for the origin of this number have been offered, none of them fully convincing, its very nature is that of six made into an absolute (three is generally the number of the divinity in Revelation), in other words a world where God is explicitly and intentionally excluded.

In the Gospel of John, interestingly, the expression "the world" has the same ambiguity as the six days of creation. The object of God's concern (see John 3:16-17; 4:42; 12:47; 17:21), the world is constantly tempted to view itself as a closed totality, and then it becomes the greatest obstacle to faith in God. In that case it is under the sway of evil (John 12:31; 14:30; 16:11) and consequently rejects Jesus and his disciples (John 7:7; 15:18-19; 17:14).

4. What do these words of Saint John mean to me: *God is light, and in him there is no darkness at all* (1 John 1:5)?
5. Am I attracted more by diversity or by unity? How can diversity be respected while remaining at the service of a more basic unity?
6. How do we exercise our responsibility for creation?
7. Where and how do we live our "Sabbaths," times to stop and remember that we are not the Source of our life?
8. Read Matthew 12:1-14. How did Jesus show the true meaning of the Sabbath?

The Garden of Delights

Genesis 2:4b begins the second account of creation, originally no doubt unconnected to the first, and formerly believed to date from an earlier age. This fact, however, should not blind us to the unity between the two strands that together form the canonical account of creation at the beginning of our Bibles. Modern research has established more and more clearly that those responsible for the final version of the Book of Genesis and the other books of Moses were much more than mere compilers seeking to juxtapose different traditions with no concern for any deeper logic. The two accounts, while quite different in form and content, complement one another admirably. Indeed, any time the Bible gives us more than one version of a key text (the Ten Words, the Beatitudes of Jesus, the Our Father, the Last Supper, etc.) this is in fact a boon, a call not to remain fixated on the "letter" of the text but to seek the inexhaustible fullness of meaning to which the different versions attempt to point, each in its own way. Such a "stereoscopic" view brings the text off the page and makes it three-dimensional, opening a space for interpretation, for our active collaboration with the Word.

In the case which now occupies us, the second account of creation completes the first in at least two areas. First of all, it is more anthropological than cosmological, focusing on the meaning and drama of human existence in the universe created by God. And second, it wrestles with the question of why the world as we know it is not identical with the "peaceable kingdom" described so compellingly in Genesis 1. Or, to put it in more general terms: Why is the handiwork of a good God not simply a realm of goodness and beauty? Why is the empirical world inferior in so many respects to what believers in a loving God would expect? Many centuries later, we are still attempting to come to grips with these questions, and so it is good to know that they were already being asked at a very early date.

If the differences between the first chapter of Genesis and the subsequent ones are highlighted in the following paragraphs, this is not primarily in order to point out the insufficiency of a literal reading of the creation story, but rather to enable us to understand better the import and meaning of the second account. Seeing it as a profound reflection on the human adventure in its own right should help us to grasp how it completes the first account, thus giving us a more profound and balanced understanding of the meaning of existence from the point of view of the inspired authors of the biblical tradition. As the first chapter of Genesis has amply demonstrated, in God's world separation or distinction can only be for the purpose of a more fundamental unity.

Thirsting for Life

Right from the start of this new account, we find ourselves in a different world. *On the day YHWH God made earth and heaven....* Not "in the beginning" or "in the course of seven days," but rather a simple "day," the Lord's Day. Not simply "God," but a God who has a proper name, the mysterious Tetragrammaton still today regarded by observant Jews as too holy to pronounce and, as far as we can make out, related to the verb "to be." Not the technical verb "to create," but the more ordinary one "to make." And finally, not "the heavens and the earth," but merely "earth and heaven." In fact, this story is more "down to earth" than the previous chapter, less a theological meditation and more like a children's tale, where unusual things happen in an everyday environment, where the supernatural reveals itself at the heart of the most mundane realities.

Next, the overarching metaphor that stands for creation is radically different, one could almost say diametrically opposed to that found in the preceding chapter. There, by God's word, dry land appeared out of the primordial waters. Here we begin with barren ground, and the act of creation involves bringing water and a cultivator into the picture. In short, it is signified by the transition from a desert to a garden. One can easily understand why people dwelling in a region where drought was a constant threat and the desert an ever encroaching presence would understand God's work as essentially that of bringing water — and thus life — into the wilderness. In the second part of the Book of Isaiah, this same metaphor is used to describe the coming time of fulfillment, which is thus implicitly viewed as a new creation:

> The poor and the needy are searching for water
> and it is not there.
> Their tongue is parched with thirst.
> I, the Lord, will answer them;
> the God of Israel, I will not leave them in the lurch.
> I will cause streams to flow on barren trails

and springs in the midst of valleys.
I will turn the wilderness into a pool of water
and the dry land into flowing springs.
I will set cedar in the wilderness,
acacia, myrtle and olive trees;
in the desert put juniper, box-trees and cypress,
that they may see and realize,
consider and understand,
that the hand of the Lord has done this,
that the Holy One of Israel created it.
          (Isaiah 41:17-20; cf. 43:19; 44:3; 45:8; 48:21; 49:10; 55:10)

In this scheme of things, de-creation is not a flood but a drying up:

By my rebuke I will dry up the sea,
make flowing streams a desert.
Fish will rot for lack of water
and die of thirst.   (Isaiah 50:2b)

Once the earth is watered, it requires a caretaker if veg-etation is to grow. Whereas chapter 1 saved the creation of humanity for the sixth day, expressing the importance of the human race by placing it at the end of a progressive series, this account accomplishes the same thing by putting *adam* at the very beginning. Verse 7 recounts this act with simple words of breathtaking profundity:

YHWH God formed the *adam* from the dirt of the ground, and blew into his nostrils the breath of life, and the *adam* became a living being.   (Genesis 2:7)

While the first chapter was marked by the ubiquitous but discreet presence of God, never confused with an inner-worldly reality and manifested only by a word from the beyond, chapter two does not hesitate to depict God in the most mundane guise imaginable. Here, God is a potter who fashions a clay vessel from the earth.

To fully appreciate the import of this sentence, we must recognize that it involves a pun, a play on words not easily rendered in translation. Indeed, this entire story works in part through language games, which were not games for the authors but showed how seriously they took words and their creative power. Unless we understand this wordplay, we often miss the point. Even when it is made explicit in an explanatory note, as in the best of our translations, we are not touched by the power of the words as we would be if we understood the original.

Literally, the text says: *YHWH God formed the* adam *from the dirt [or dust] of the* adamah.... By this simple pun, which establishes a verbal link between "man" and the soil, the author expresses a truth which could be expanded into pages of philosophical anthropology. For the Bible human beings belong to this earth; they are part and parcel of creation. They are not, as in some other worldviews, strangers in a strange land, beings parachuted down to earth in a previous age and constantly looking for a way back to their true homeland. Salvation, therefore, does not involve a repudiation of the good things of this world.

This correspondence also highlights the fragile nature of human beings. Made of mere dust and then endowed by their Creator with impressive gifts, the principal one being life itself, they are constantly in danger of returning to the almost-nothingness from which they came. By themselves they cannot ensure their survival and the quality of their existence. Another word used by the Bible to express the fragile, limited nature of human beings is the word "flesh." A text which also comes from Second

Isaiah uses this expression to reaffirm the insight of Genesis 2:7. The prophet, seemingly in despair, at first cries out:

> All flesh is grass
> and all its grace like the wild flowers.
> The grass dries up, the flowers wither....
>
> (Isaiah 40:6-7a)

But then comes the encouraging response:

> The grass dries up, the flowers wither,
> but the word of our God endures forever.
>
> (Isaiah 40:8)

And indeed, if *adam* is inescapably dust of this earth, this does not exhaustively define his identity. Human beings are at home in this world, yet not quite at home. To finish making them what they are meant to be, in addition to being formed from the soil, they receive something directly from God, *a breath of life*.[10] They are not just beings who are simply part of this world; in them there is the aspiration to something greater. This explains why, though we normally need the good things of this world to live a gratifying life, these things will never make us fully content. There always remains an underlying dissatisfaction that no earthly reality can still. How can we not think here of the haunting words of Saint Augustine: "You have made us for yourself, O God, and our hearts can never rest until they rest in you" (*Confessions* I, 1)?

---

[10] The word for breath here is *neshamah* and not the more usual *ruah*, perhaps to maintain a certain distance between humans and God; the author may be unwilling to imply that the former are animated directly by the Spirit of God. Nonetheless the two words are synonyms, and so the basic affirmation holds.

Through this conjunction between the dust of the earth and God's breath of life, a *living being* arises. The word translated "being" here, *nephesh*, first of all refers to the throat or the upper thorax. It is sometimes translated as "soul," but this category, more familiar to us from the Greco-Roman tradition, may mislead us into conceiving a more ethereal reality than is in fact the case. The *nephesh* is the locus where things from the outside are taken into the body in order to make life possible — first of all air, then food and drink. It therefore depicts humans as beings who are not autonomous, self-sufficient, but creatures who live in symbiosis with the rest of the universe. Consequently, it expresses the fact that humans are beings of desire, who long for what they do not possess. It is extremely significant that, whereas the Greco-Roman tradition tends to see rationality as the characteristic mark of human beings, the Bible defines human life as inherently rooted in a longing, an aspiration for greater life. As opposed to animals locked into their instincts, humans are constantly searching to go beyond what is given; they possess a fundamental openness to the unknown. For good or ill, they are inhabited by a dynamism which leads them where they never imagined they would go.

The Garden of God

Once God has brought water to the dry ground and created a being to till the soil, he plants a garden so that the earthling can accomplish this task. We should note in passing that, although in chapter 1 *adam* can be taken merely as a collective noun, "humankind," here things are more complicated because of the literary form employed, that of a story. *Ha-adam*, which can be translated as "the earthling" to attempt to capture the play on words mentioned above, is both an individual man (on the level of the story) and humanity in general (on the level of the story's meaning). Both levels need to be held together for the significance of the text to be rightly grasped. This was not difficult for the Semitic peoples of old, thanks to the notion of the eponymous ancestor: the founder of a nation or collectivity in some sense represents the entire group. Israel, for example, is both an alternate name for the patriarch Jacob and the name of the nation issued from his seed. The Israelites, in biblical terminology, are "the sons (or children) of Israel," and the son is in the image of the father (cf. Genesis 5:3). Thus it was a very short step for the hearers of this story to view *adam* as simultaneously the first human being in a series and as a "collective personality" who in some sense stands for each one of us.[11]

God plants a garden, then, and places the earthling in it. Although in some sense the step is the natural prolongation of this story, in which creation is conceived as the movement from a sterile waste to flourishing vegetation, at the same time the image of the garden takes us beyond the world as we know it. It does not merely depict things as they are. It is not hard to see why,

---

[11] In his Letter to the Romans, Saint Paul is an heir to this outlook. In 5:12ff, Adam is the *one human being* through whom sin came into the world but, in Paul's mind, Adam is not just one individual among others. He is the first man who recapitulates in himself the fate of all of his descendants, *insofar as all have sinned* (5:12b). Thus, later on (7:7ff), Paul has no qualms about using the first-person pronoun ("I") to express Adam's situation: *I was once alive when there was no law, but when the commandment came, sin came to life* (7:9). In a mysterious but very real sense, Adam is each of us and each of us is Adam. This way of thinking, of course, gives the apostle an ideal opportunity to explain the relationship of Christ Jesus to us, and to answer the question of how the fate of "one human being" can bring salvation to the many. For him Christ too is not just an individual, but the firstborn of a new creation (cf. 8:29; Colossians 1:18); we are his body (12:5).

for the inhabitants of the Middle East, a region often threatened by drought, a beautiful garden teeming with all sorts of plant life would represent an ideal world. It is not for nothing that, in the Persian language, the word "paradise" simply means "an enclosed garden." Likewise, the word *eden* can mean "something lavish, luxurious; a delight." And in the mythology of that part of the world, the motif of "God's garden" (cf. Isaiah 51:3; Ezekiel 28:13) shows up in various places, before resurfacing, centuries later, in the literature of Islam. As in the first account of creation, therefore, the world as it comes from God's hands is not merely identical with the empirical universe as we know it. The rest of the story will attempt to explain this discrepancy.

The garden contains *every tree desirable to look at and good for food* (2:9). Once again, in this account of creation the logic is anthropocentric: the plants are created for human beings, and this is expressed chronologically, by the fact that they appear after the earthling in the story. The vegetation is a feast both for the eyes and for the stomach, and here we already find the seeds of a possible division: what the eyes see and desire is not necessarily what is good to satisfy our needs.

At the center of the garden stands *the tree of life*. Its central position defines in some sense the meaning of the whole garden, and therefore of existence. What better way to express the conviction that God desires to give to creation the fullness of life? Here we are in direct continuity with the words of Jesus in John 10:10: *I have come that they may have life, and have it to the full.* The story goes on to highlight this theme by returning to the image of water, which already has been presented as the "energy" which makes creation possible. From the garden flows a stream which feeds the four great rivers of humanity. Eden is thus not situated in a fairy-tale world with no relationship to our earth; the author wishes to emphasize the continuity between the garden and the history of our world. Whatever is truly alive and life-sustaining in our existence, he seems to say, has its roots in God and in the divine act of creation. We find a similar notion in the prophet Ezekiel's vision of the future, where water flows from the reconstructed Temple and turns the world into a beautiful garden (Ezekiel 47:6-12), a motif taken up in the very last chapter of the Christian Bible (Revelation 22:1-2).[12] The beginning and end of history correspond, and this is to be expected insofar as both bring us into contact with the Source.

One Tree or Two?

In our description of the garden of delights, we passed over a detail which will be of major importance for the development of the story. The words ...*and the tree of the knowledge of good and evil* (2:9b) have all the earmarks of a later addition that disturbs the harmony of the picture. By definition, only one object can be in the middle of a given space, and indeed, it is not clear whether the author's intention is to speak of two trees, or of a single tree with two different names. It is as if a mythological description of "the garden of God" has been transformed, by the addition of this detail, into the beginning of a parable with dramatic interest. The inspired author plants a seed that will al-

---

[12] The Fourth Gospel also takes up this motif. Jesus comes to offer *living water*, so that the one who accepts it will never be thirsty again (John 4:10, 14). At a key moment he cries out: *Let whoever is thirsty come to me and drink. As Scripture says, Out of him will flow streams of living water* which the evangelist links to the gift of the Spirit at Jesus' glorification (7:37-39). Finally, we see the fulfillment of this prophecy on the cross, when water flows out of the Crucified One's side along with blood (19:31-37).

low a plot to take shape, that will make a story — indeed history as such — possible.

It is therefore crucial to understand better the significance of the expression *the tree of the knowledge of good and evil*. Before examining the vocabulary, we should say a word about the wider context, the horizon of interpretation. Among all the biblical texts, these chapters of Genesis have been among the most widely read and commented upon. The history of interpretation already begins in the Hebrew Scriptures themselves and continues in the New Testament and beyond, down to the present day. Genesis 1-4 thus appears in fact as a huge nebula, a cloud with the texts themselves at the core. This means that we already approach these texts with many preconceptions. It is virtually impossible to read them in a naïve or straightforward fashion, as if for the first time. This is not to say, of course, that the many commentaries on these passages that have arisen over centuries are necessarily deformations or perversions of the original meaning. Here as elsewhere, we need to be wary of the prejudice, unfortunately so widespread in our day, that the earliest version or interpretation is the most authentic. In many cases, subsequent reflections elucidate and even deepen the meaning of the original text. But at times the preconceived notions that these later perspectives foster in us form a kind of filter that keeps us from grasping the true import of the story. This is so not so much on account of the details of the interpretation as because of the all-encompassing worldview of the interpreters, their unexamined assumptions. It is good and at times even necessary, then, to become aware of the readings that are in danger of keeping us from seeing what the story is in fact trying to tell us, so that we can gain a certain distance from them.

In these pages I will mention two such readings that prevent many people today from grasping the point of our story. Let us call the first of these "the moralistic reading." Genesis 2-3 admittedly confronts the question "Why is the world as we know it different from the world as God wishes it to be?" and the answer it suggests has to do with human choices and behavior. In this sense, the story obviously has a moral dimension. In the course of the ages, however, the center of gravity shifted in line with a changing understanding of the Christian faith, whereby sin — and not divine grace — began implicitly to be considered as the motive force of history.[13] So many commentators and preachers have taken the text as a particularly telling example of human depravity that its primary purpose came to be seen as that of creating guilt feelings, not to say self-loathing, in the hearers. In our day, there is a strong and understandable allergic reaction to such a perspective on the part of many, which extends even to the vocabulary used, so that unfortunately the baby of the text is often thrown out with the bathwater of the moralistic interpretation.

The misunderstanding begins here, with the expression mentioned above. Hearing the words "good and evil," we focus on "evil," which evokes for us sin, guilt, hellfire and all the rest. Even a cursory examination of the expression in the Bible, however, invalidates such an interpretation. The Semitic languages often use pairs of opposites when they wish to indicate a totality. When Jesus says to the disciples in John's Gospel, for example,

---

[13] The complex question of how a faith originally proclaimed as "good news" of humanity's salvation came to be seen by many, particularly in the West, as a moralistic condemnation of human behavior, and even an enemy of life, would make a fascinating study in itself.

If you forgive anyone's sins they are forgiven; if you retain them they are retained (John 20:23; cf. Matthew 16:19), he is telling them that they have full and ultimate powers to declare forgiveness in God's name. The accent is not on the refusal to offer forgiveness, but on the complete authority given by Jesus to his disciples. The two opposites — here, to forgive and to retain — cover the whole semantic field in question.

Analogously, then, the expression "good and evil" means, in simple terms, "everything that has to do with behavior." Something of this meaning is still present in the English expression "to know right from wrong" (cf. Isaiah 7:15-16), with the difference, however, that the Hebrew words are not limited to moral behavior in the narrow meaning of the term. They refer rather to knowing the right or wrong way to act in any situation where human lives are affected, involving both moral and practical decisions.

"The tree of the knowledge of good and evil," then, is the tree of knowing how to live in the right way, to lead a life that is as it should be. There is a biblical word, one not however mentioned in this text, which sums up this kind of knowledge; that word is **wisdom**. Wisdom in the Bible is not some kind of esoteric lore or abstract book-learning; it is the essentially practical ability to discern in any situation what favors life and what diminishes it. On one level it is not far from what today we call "common sense," the ability to make the choices that lead to a life which is happy, fulfilled, successful and productive. Wisdom is what provides the answer to the question "What is the good life?" and does so not primarily in abstract terms, but by helping people to make the concrete choices that make such a life possible.

And now we can perhaps understand why these two trees

are together in the center of God's garden, to the point that they
may even be one and the same tree. The story tells us that, for
human beings, life is inseparable from the ability to know *how*
to live. As opposed to animal existence, human life is not simply
a given, a series of innate programs, called instincts, that operate
in large part automatically. If our life is to be worth living, to be
what God wants it to be, we need to make the right choices, and
therefore we need to know how to make them. The search for
wisdom is the overarching theme of several biblical books, and
it seems to be an overriding concern of this story as well.

The Human Project

Verse 15 repeats the statement that God places the earthling
in a beautiful garden, adding these words: ...*to till it and take
care of it*. Whereas in the first account of creation, the role of
human beings in the world was defined by a verb taken from
the political domain, *to have dominion* (1:26), here the same
idea is expressed in a humbler register: the *adam* is basically a
cultivator or gardener. The first verb used, "to till," is one that
refers to human labor, and it tells us that, in its essence, work
was intended by God from the very beginning to be part of the
human vocation. Not simply a harsh necessity, still less a punishment, work is seen here as a way of sharing in God's own
creative activity. It is something positive, a great responsibility
by which human beings are called to shape the still "unfinished"
earth. This is reinforced by the second verb used, translated as
"to take care of" but also meaning "to watch over." Humanity is
asked to keep an eye on the rest of creation, so to speak, making sure it remains faithful to its God-given identity. In biblical

terms, we are called to do what is necessary so that the entire universe may give glory to God.

Following this general description of the human project, God now speaks for the first time to the earthling he has created. And his first words are an order or command. Again we are asked to leave behind a moralistic reading of the story, which would seize upon this detail to justify an image of God as a dictator interested above all in controlling his subjects and limiting their freedom. The true import of God's speaking can only be grasped if we return to the central theme of our story — the search for wisdom.

Wisdom was defined above as the answer to the question "What is the good life?" To some extent an answer to this question can be found by personal reflection, but a more effective way, and one more commonly proposed in the Bible, is by listening to the advice of more experienced people, who have taken the wisdom of their ancestors and enriched it by their own trials and errors. Thus a large part of the so-called Wisdom literature in the Bible consists of maxims that are handed down from one generation to the next:

> Listen, children, to a father's correction,
> and try and understand how to be intelligent.
> For I have given you good instruction;
> do not forsake my teaching.
> For I was a son to my father,
> pampered as my mother's only son.
> He taught me, saying:
> Hold my words in your heart;
> do what I tell you and you will live.   (Proverbs 4:1-4)

Do what I tell you and you will live. This advice of a father to his children is far from a narrow moralistic outlook and applies equally well — and indeed better — to the first words of God in Genesis 2. They are to be rightly understood as authoritative instruction to the children of God regarding how to attain true life and happiness on this earth. After all, who better than the Creator should know "the ground rules," the basic orientations which will enable human beings to make the best use of their potentialities?

God's command, the key to achieving the good life, has in fact two parts. This is usually overlooked by the moralistic reading, which leaps immediately to the second, negative part of the injunction and sees it as more essential, since it seems to validate the image of a deity whose only concern is to frustrate the authentic desires of human beings. In point of fact, the first command given by God is a positive one:

> Of all the trees of the garden you may freely eat.
> (Genesis 2:16)

God begins by telling the *adam* to use and enjoy the good things at his disposal, to make use of his liberty to ameliorate his life. Far from attempting to curtail human freedom, the first words of God set this freedom at the heart of what it means to be human. Human beings are invited to develop their potential fully; they are not mere robots programmed to behave in a certain way. But although an infinite number of choices lie open before them, a moment's reflection should tell us that they cannot exercise them all at once. In the terms of the story, the earthling may well have access to all the trees, but of which of them should he eat at any given moment? The possibilities may well be unlimited, but the being who is encouraged to make use of them is not. So once again the story leads us back to the basic question of wisdom: what are the true priorities, the choices that will make authentic life a reality?

This question, which is hidden behind the first part of God's command, becomes explicit in the second part. The "yes" is followed by a "but no":

> But of the tree of the knowledge of good and evil you
> may not eat....   (Genesis 2:17a)

The limit inherent in every choice is openly expressed here, and projected on to one particular tree. Looked at from without, this command seems simply an arbitrary limitation of human freedom, and indeed no explanation is given as the motive for it. Instead, God mentions the consequences:

> ...because on the day you eat of it you will surely die.
>   (Genesis 2:17b)

In the moralistic reading this is interpreted as a punishment, all the more intolerable because the command appears arbitrary. The text itself, however, gives no reason not to take these words rather as a warning of the consequences which will inevitably follow from the activity in question. And if we discover one day that the command was not arbitrary, then this second possibility becomes much more plausible. Sending her little children out into the backyard, mother says, "You can play anywhere in the yard you like, but do not go out of the yard and play in the street, for on the day you do that you will surely die." What is meant as a warning of probable consequences may well be interpreted by the children as a threat: "If mother catches us going out into the street, she will kill us!"

Limits: Good or Bad?

Let us now look more closely at God's command. At first all the trees are given for food, then one tree is excluded. This is not, incidentally, the indication of an afterthought on God's part, but rather a Semitic form of expression: the whole is first mentioned, and then the details that modify it.[14] In any case, the second part of the command sets an explicit limit. This bothers us, and indeed there is something in us that would prefer a world in which everything is possible, and straightaway. That, however, is not the world we live in. The founder of psychoanalysis, Sigmund Freud, distinguished between the "pleasure principle" of immediate gratification and the "reality principle," necessary for human beings to learn in order to function in society. The biblical author in his turn, by modifying God's gift of all of the trees with the injunction not to eat from one of them, brings the story into line with the human condition, with the "real world" in which we live. In that world, as opposed to our fantasies, our freedom is not unlimited.

There are different kinds of limits set to human freedom, and not only moral ones. First, there are the limits that arise from the nature of the physical world. Children might want to consume only chocolate and soft drinks, but their parents know that they must eat their vegetables and drink their milk if they are to remain healthy. And if someone were to decide to limit their diet to grass and petroleum, then the experiment would be even shorter. "If you eat these things, you will surely die."

Second, there are limits occasioned by the fact that I am

---

[14] Cf., among many other examples, John 1:11-12: *He came to his own, and his own did not welcome him. But to those who did welcome him....* The latter group presumably includes some of "his own," the Jewish people.

not alone in the universe. I must take other beings into account. Johnny sees the chocolate cake mother has made and wants all of it, but so does his sister Barbara. So the children must be encouraged to share; if one of them eats it all, there is nothing left for the other one. Similarly, God's command situates me in a world with other people who do not merely exist in function of me. Our limits are a reminder of the existence of the other, who must be taken into account if life together is to continue.

Another sort of limit concerns our knowledge. Most of us have never been to New Zealand. And yet we are absolutely convinced that a place called New Zealand exists on this earth. But perhaps it is all a great hoax. Perhaps the *Lord of the Rings* films were made in New Jersey, using special effects entirely done on a computer. Our knowledge is inevitably built upon faith in what others communicate to us. We can only deconstruct this up to a certain point, and then again probably not without the help of others. What we know from direct experience is only an infinitesimal part of the sum of our knowledge.

All the types of limits just mentioned are signs of our creatureliness. We are not ourselves the source of life; we need what is beyond our own selves in order to survive. But there is another kind of limit, those we consciously choose for a greater purpose. Here we enter the realm of morality proper. Some people choose to limit their consumption so that others are able to live. They may buy a car that consumes less gas, or products made by companies that do not exploit their workers. Or they choose to earn less money so they have more time for volunteer service. Such choices, when made wholeheartedly, witness to the fact that accepting certain limits to one's behavior does not impair the ability to live a good life. They show that the road to true happiness does not involve divesting oneself of all constraints.

These limitations freely chosen or accepted are not a sign of creatureliness. In the biblical vision of the world, God at times chooses to limit his own power with a view to a greater good. God's omnipotence does not entail imposing the divine will upon human beings against their own wishes. God acts by means of his word, which calls out to us and invites us to enter into a relationship. To put it another way, the divine power is the power of love, and love never forces the loved one to accept this love.

This self-limitation, already adumbrated in the Hebrew Scriptures, is seen most strikingly in the person of Jesus in the New Testament. An ancient Christian hymn taken up by Paul in his Letter to the Philippians expresses it clearly:

> Although his condition was divine,
> he did not consider being equal to God
> an exclusive right
> but emptied himself,
> taking on the condition of a slave. (Philippians 2:6-7a)

Being God does not mean striving at all costs to possess everything; God lives rather by giving and receiving, and asks us to do the same. And it is our limits that make this possible. The frontier that separates what is us from what is not us defines us and the other, and thus opens the door to relationship.

Receiving from an Other

In the real world, then, freedom and happiness are not found in the total absence of limits. And in Genesis 2, the negative side of God's words set the limit within which this freedom and happiness can blossom. But why this particular limit? Is not the command not to eat the fruit of one specific tree simply an arbitrary and therefore unjust limitation of human freedom?

In fact, the tree forbidden by God is not merely one tree among all the others chosen at random. It is "the tree of the knowledge of good and evil," the shadow of the tree of life at the center of the garden. Since this tree, as we have seen, provides the answer to the question "What is the good life?" then the divine commandment represents a warning to human beings not to arrogate this knowledge to themselves. Taking the fruit from this tree is a symbolic expression of the attempt to possess the secret of life, and thus implicitly to see oneself as the Source. The act is not forbidden because there is something wrong with the tree and its fruit, or because God wishes to torture or test his creature or keep back the best for himself. The double tree remains at the center of the garden, giving meaning to everything in it, defining the garden as the space given to humans so that they can find true life and happiness. God is therefore not attempting to deprive the earthling either of life or of the road to get there, but rather closing off an illusory and dangerous route. You may do whatever you think best in order to live out your calling to take care of the garden for me, God says in effect, but you must never forget that your life and the knowledge of how to live it come from me. If and when you do forget this, and begin to imagine that you yourselves are the source of these goods, then the self-created world you fantasize can, since it is unreal, only lead to death.

God's prohibition, therefore, does more than simply setting a limit to behavior and thus opening a space for the discovery of the other. It obliges human beings to take into account that primary Other whom we call God. At the center of our existence there is an empty space of not-knowing, to which access is found only by trust in an Other who is the Source of all knowledge. We may ask all the questions we like, and keep searching to expand the bounds of our knowledge, but what we must not forget is that our answers, in the final analysis, can only be received as a gift in response to our searching. Understanding and wisdom are not absolutes but are rooted in a relationship, a fundamental openness to the Ground of our being.

It is highly significant that the very same structure traced out by God's words in Genesis 2 is replicated in the Ten Words, which have at their center the injunction to observe the Sabbath (see Exodus 20:8-11; Deuteronomy 5:12-15). At the close of the week there is a day which is an "empty space," where believers are asked to stop and remember that the entire week is a gift from God. This "useless" day is in fact the key to the entire week, since it is a reminder of where everything comes from and where it is all heading. In the same way, the tree(s) at the center of the garden, which are off-limits to human beings and not under their control, allow the entire garden to remain in existence and to be what it truly is. In traditional language, we have here in essence the category of the "sacred" or the "holy": if any human society is to survive, it must recognize an Origin that is surrounded with respect and not subject to human manipulation. The fact that modern society has no way of making sense of this category from within its own presuppositions places it in a unique dilemma: if nothing is sacred, then what is to stop us in the end from sawing off the branch upon which we are sitting?[15]

---

[15]   See Brother John of Taizé, *The Adventure of Holiness* (New York: ST PAULS/Alba House, 1999).

God's words to the *adam*, then, express in the simplest of terms the basic structure of human existence. It involves the freedom to make use of the good things of creation in order to attain the fullness of life. This freedom has only one limit, but it is an all-important one: humans must remember that they are not the Source of life, that they receive it as a gift from an Other. Limits, the other, and gift: these three notions are thus shown to be intimately related, and together they sketch out the essential features of what it means to be human.

Made for Communion

With the divine command, then, the question of the other has arisen: my limits indicate the place where I can go no further. They set a boundary around me which distinguishes me from what is not me, and thus make relationship possible and necessary. Now this theme will be treated explicitly, in a short fable dealing with the creation of the sexes.

The passage begins with God speaking to himself. And for the first time in the Bible, something is defined as *not good*. This is all the more striking since in chapter one, everything created by God was expressly described as *good*, indeed *very good*. Now, however, something is considered an obstacle to the good life given by God.

The obstacle to fulfillment is *to be alone*. Indirectly but explicitly, we are thus told that the normal condition of human beings is companionship. Here the Bible states clearly what is manifest on all of its pages: human beings need others to live a life which is worth living. Aloneness is not the state that characterizes our race. This does not mean, of course, that times of solitude are not important, indeed essential, in order to be ourselves and to seek that Other who is God. Nonetheless, our basic identity is found in and through relationship. In these words of God, we have something similar to what Genesis 1 attempted to express by associating the image of God with the creation of humans as male and female.

It is worth pausing for a moment to reflect upon how this biblical understanding of the human condition is different from what people instinctively believe in the West today. For centuries now, we have been conditioned to see the human being as basically an individual, someone who finds his or her identity in a self which is prior to, and essentially independent from, the influences that come from without. This modern self is, of course, largely a fiction. It would be far truer to say that what we call the self is born and maintained by constant inter- action with the non-human and human environment. It does not spring into being full-blown, like Minerva from the head of Jupiter. And yet we persist in believing that our opinions and decisions are exclusively the fruit of our own striving, and that we consequently have an inalienable right to them. Of course we cannot deny our true nature completely, and so we practice a diffuse gregariousness that momentarily assuages our thirst for a shared life. Since this is not rooted in the self, however, which jealously protects its splendid isolation, such superficial togeth- erness does not in the end prove satisfying. We wonder why we have such trouble maintaining relationships of any depth, why our marriages and friendships do not last, while at the same time we flee any limitation of our sovereign self through authentic commitment. If we are indeed self-made men (and women), then logically the question of the other does not arise in any seriously meaningful way.

The biblical vision is quite different, and indeed diametrically opposed to this outlook. In the story we are examining, God acts to remedy the unreal condition of an isolated being, so contrary to the divine intention for creation. *I will make him an* ezēr *kenegedo* (2:18). The translation of this expression is particularly perilous, for reasons which have little to do with the text itself. Earlier, we examined an interpretation of Genesis 2-3 which I termed the moralistic reading and which makes it hard for us to grasp the true intentions of the inspired author. Another such interpretation, which also has exercised its ravages down through the ages, is what we can call the misogynistic reading. It discerns in the text an affirmation of the superiority of the male and a denigration of the female. Not surprisingly, in this case too the tendency has been to throw out the baby with the bathwater. In fact, today the misogynistic reading seems paradoxically more alive and well than ever, albeit in an inverted form: it is assumed as indisputable truth that the second creation story offers an anthropology humiliating to women, and so it is rejected out of hand.

What evidence for this reading do we find in the text itself? The Authorized Version translates the expression as *a help meet for him*; the NRSV *a helper as his partner.* It is the word *ezēr,* "help(er)," which first seems to provide ammunition for the misogynistic reading and is therefore rejected by those wishing to fight against sexism. Both sides, while disagreeing on their acceptance of what they consider the biblical teaching, nonetheless understand the word in the same way. In their minds *ezēr* means "assistant," someone in an inferior position who takes on those distasteful but necessary tasks which those in power would rather not waste their time on. In a society where women have often played that role, people can perhaps be forgiven for understanding *ezēr* as the equivalent of "dishwasher, typist, housekeeper" and so forth.

There is one main problem with this interpretation. In the Bible, outside of Genesis 2:18, *ezēr* is used primarily to refer to God! The word is found several times in the Psalms:

> I raise my eyes to the mountains:
> where will my help come from?
> My help comes from the Lord,
> the Maker of heaven and earth.
>
> (Psalm 121:2; cf. 124:8; 146:5)

Its meaning is therefore "someone who supplies what is lacking and thus makes it possible for me to become who I truly should be." The word has absolutely no connotations of inequality. If anything, the *ezēr* is in a more favorable position than the one who asks for and receives the aid, because the former has what the latter is lacking. The next word, however, defines more clearly the kind of relationship God will create. *Kenegedo* means literally "over against, in front of, face to face" and seems to be used in this context to express the equality of the relationship. This "help" is neither inferior nor superior; it corresponds to the *adam*. It is what the earthling needs to fulfill his vocation, to become who he really is. In short, God's words here, understood correctly, offer no justification for the misogynistic reading. The problem is human aloneness; the solution is an *ezēr kenegedo*, a being whose very existence would solve the problem, in a word a companion.

A Fit Companion

Who is a fit companion for the *adam*? The text does not answer the question abstractly, but in story form. First, God forms all the other living beings from the *adamah*, and brings them to the *adam* to receive their name. Here we see another difference from Genesis 1: the animals are created after the human being.[16] They are fashioned in the same way by God from the ground, but are not explicitly said to receive a breath of life directly from their Creator. Their difference is shown in another way as well: the *adam* has the task of giving them a name. Names in traditional cultures, and so in the Bible, are far more than mere labels. A name expresses someone's identity, thus giving them a place in the world. It can be said that until they receive a name, the different beings do not fully exist. The earthling's God-given task, therefore, is to collaborate in God's work of creation by the use of language. Here the *adam* is placed, so to speak, on the divine side of the divide between the Creator and the creatures, by being attributed a role that belongs by right to God. Once again we see the intermediate status of human beings, already sketched out in Genesis 2:7 and reinforced by the assigned task of watching over the garden (Genesis 2:15): they are part of creation, and at the same time more than this. This intermediate status means that they can go in either direction, and so gives to their existence a dramatic character which neither God nor the animals share.

All the living beings created by God and named by the

---

[16] This may explain in part why Genesis 1 appears more "modern" to us, so that it has usually been considered as more recent. It follows the same progression as today's evolutionary biology: plants > animals > humans. Genesis 2, on the other hand, offers a counter-intuitive and decidedly anthropocentric scheme: human being > plants > animals > woman/man.

adam are implicitly considered as good, but none of them is an *ezēr kenegedo*, a fit companion for him. The story has thus set up a dramatic tension which must be resolved by a new act of God. God's first step is to put the earthling to sleep; the act will therefore be purely divine, with no human collaboration. But the text goes further: the word used here is not the ordinary word for sleep, but something closer to our word "torpor," a state of insensibility which is not part of the ordinary rhythm of the human life cycle. In essence, then, things go back to the beginning, to the moment of the *adam's* creation. In this way the story expresses the fact that an authentic new beginning is taking place, and that what is about to happen has the same importance as the creation of the *adam* in 2:7. Expressed in somewhat extreme fashion, we could say that God starts all over again to eliminate what was "not good" in his first attempt. For those able to see the text without the blinders of the misogynistic interpretation, there is no subordination here.

Next, God takes the side (or the rib, both translations are possible) of the earthling and builds it into an *isshah*, a woman. Just as the *adam's* creation by God directly from the *adamah* demonstrated, not the inferiority of the earthling to the ground from which it came but the essential relationship linking the two, so here the direct creation of the woman from the side of the *adam* shows not inequality but a special intimate relationship, fundamentally different from all the other relationships between the *adam* and the other living beings. The somewhat surprising use of the verb "to build" here is another of those plays on words so beloved of our author: the Hebrew idiom "to build a woman" means to give her children, to found a family. In creating the *isshah*, God ensures that life will continue.

God then takes the *isshah* and brings her to the *adam*. Instead of a simple naming, now there is a cry of recognition and joy. *This one this time is bone of my bone and flesh of my flesh!* (Genesis 2:23a). The expression is normally used in the Bible to state that two persons belong to the same family or ethnic group (see Genesis 29:14; 2 Samuel 5:1). Unlike the animals, then, this new being is both other than the *adam*, and the same; she is thus a fit companion for him. And through the encounter with this *alter ego*, this other self, human speech, as opposed to mere naming, comes into being. There is now the possibility — and the need — to communicate, to enter into an authentic relationship. The problem of loneliness is solved.

The next words are unfortunately incomprehensible in most of our translations, because they are based on another word-play:

> This one will be called *isshah*, for from *ish* was taken
> this one. (Genesis 2:23b)

The process of naming the new creature emphasizes the aforementioned parallel with the first creation of the earthling: *adam* from *adamah* and *isshah* from *ish*.[17] But another detail is worthy of notice, and it also is not usually conveyed by the translations. Up to now, the human creature created by God has been called only "the earthling," *ha-adam*, traditionally translated by "(the) man." And these same Bibles usually translate verse 23b as *This one will be called woman, for out of man was this one taken*. But the word translated "man" here is not *adam* but *ish*, a new word which appears for the first time and refers

---

[17] In reality, the two words *ish* and *isshah* come from different roots; what we have here is an example of folk etymology. But this fact has absolutely no importance for the meaning of the story, which is founded not on a supposed scientific truth but on the perception of the hearers.

explicitly to the male human being. What we could never discover from these translations is the fact that, when the woman comes into being, the earthling receives a new name. Now a new name, in the Bible, is always significant; it expresses a new identity, usually after an encounter that marks someone for life (cf. Genesis 32:28). So in a very real sense, it would be fair to say that we are witnessing the creation of not one but two new beings: *isshah* comes into existence, and as a result *adam* is manifested as *ish*.

The text thus reveals a truth of paramount importance, valid beyond the specific male-female duality: we need others to find our own identity, to become who we really are. Once again the Bible challenges an individualistic mindset which imagines the "self" as given from the start. On the contrary, our self is formed by and through the contact with the other, the primordial Other being God. As a Zulu proverb puts it, "A person is a person through other people."[18] The undifferentiated earthling is now the couple *ish-isshah*, whereby each knows him- or herself through the encounter with the other.

It may be helpful to stop for a moment and meditate on the significance of what we have just seen. If we are able to lay aside the prejudices with which we habitually regard this passage, we can discover a view of human beings, an anthropology, which is of astonishing depth and still as relevant today as it was thousands of years ago. In this account, one has become two without ceasing to be one. The creation of *isshah* adds nothing extra to *ha-adam* — she is not an appendage, or even a comple-

---

[18] Quoted in Helen Epstein, "The Lost Children of AIDS," *The New York Review of Books*, November 3, 2005, p. 42. This is the basis of the African notion of *ubuntu,* interrelationship among humans.

ment — but rather her coming into existence makes *ha-adam*, humanity, fully real, fully what it is, since one being in isolation is not humanity. She is thus the "help" in the fullest sense of the term. The curse of aloneness, with death as its implicit corollary, is removed, and ongoing life is henceforth possible. A sterile unity, that of a detached unit, is replaced by a fertile, life-giving one — a union expressed in and through relationship.

As a consequence of this, the account of woman's creation closes with a programmatic statement, one which has had great significance in the ongoing tradition:

> For this reason an *ish* leaves his father and his mother
> and clings to his *isshah*, and they become one flesh.
>
> (Genesis 2:24)

This text is taken up at two key moments in the New Testament, in Matthew 19:5, when Jesus gives his teaching on marriage and divorce, and in Ephesians 5:31, when Saint Paul speaks of marriage as a sign or parable of Christ and the Church. It justifies the marriage bond as corresponding to the intimate nature of human beings. In this sense it forms an inclusion with the first verse of the subsection: if human beings are made not for solitude but for relationship (v. 18), then this is why couples are formed. It should be pointed out that the expression *to become one flesh* does not refer primarily to the sexual act, as moderns tend to imagine. It means rather "one new human reality" and refers to the creation of a new cell in the body of humankind — the couple and then the nuclear family.

Another curious feature of the verse is that it is the male who leaves home and attaches himself to the female. This was not the custom in Israel in historic times. Does the verse originally go back to a prehistoric matrilocal family structure? In any event, it would not be wrong to conclude that, at the time Genesis 2 was set down in writing, its intention was to describe not a material change of residence, but the inner journey of a person. That is represented here by the male, precisely because he does not usually go to live with his wife's family. Marriage is a true new beginning, involving a break with an old life (represented by father and mother[19]) and the creation of a new and definitive bond. In this sense it has the same structure as the relationship with God: Abraham is called to leave home and kin to embark upon an adventure with the Lord (cf. Genesis 12:1-4), and many centuries later, some ordinary fishermen leave family and occupation to set out on the roads of Galilee with Jesus (cf. Mark 1:16-20). Interestingly, in Deuteronomy 11:22, we find the same verb "to cling" used to describe the relationship which the believer is called to establish with God. The story of the creation of woman, then, began with a oneness that was not good ("alone"), only to end with a oneness that is good ("one flesh") because it does not deny the other. And to reach this oneness which includes diversity, a kind of dying to the old is necessary so that a new beginning is possible. The human journey is thus defined as a journey towards communion, involving a death and a resurrection.

---

[19] "Leaving father and mother" does not mean repudiating or neglecting them, but rather leaving behind the passive status of an immature child to assume one's own responsibilities in life. See Brother John of Taizé, *Reading the Ten Commandments Anew*, pp. 55-58.

Questions for Reflection

1. In what ways do I feel part of this world? In what ways do I feel like a stranger on this earth?

2. In Genesis 2, Paradise is described as a beautiful garden. What gives **me** joy and happiness in life? What diminishes my happiness?

3. Have I been influenced by a moralistic reading of the Bible? What allows me to discover instead a God who is a Giver and who wants the fullness of life for his creatures? How is this compatible with the divine commandments?

4. Does the image of a gardener offer a good way of understanding our responsibility for the planet? In what ways can we cultivate the earth? How can our work be a means of collaborating with God?

5. Can limitations ever be something positive? What enables me to accept my limits?

6. "Human beings are created for community, not solitude." Do I agree with this statement? Why or why not? What does Genesis 2 help us to understand about the relationship between men and women, and indeed about all human relationships?

A Clash of Wisdoms

With the replacement of the undifferentiated *adam* by the couple *isshah-ish*, the world of Genesis 2-3 comes to resemble more closely the empirical world in which we live. What gives our life its drama is not solely the search for the key to correct living — wisdom — in relationship to the Source of existence and to the material world, but, just as importantly, the attempt to make our way in a world where we are not alone. Wisdom entails knowing how to live in harmony with the other human beings who people our planet. As we know from personal experience, we can either help or hinder one another on the road to authentic life. Our story will now work out the theme of true wisdom in all its varied dimensions.

Chapter 2 of the Book of Genesis closes with the statement: *The* adam *and his* isshah *were both naked and did not feel ashamed.*[20] Nudity may suggest to us things as different as

---

[20] I have placed this transitional verse with chapter 3 because of the inclusion with v. 7: the notion of nakedness frames, as it were, the story of temptation and the consent to it. Notice that in this verse, where one might expect the words "the *ish* and his *isshah*" we have instead "the *adam* and his *isshah*." On the level of the story, *ha-adam* ("the earthling") denotes the original creature present in the garden. And this creature does not split into two new beings to form man and woman, as in some myths of an original hermaphrodite humanity, but receives a new and more specific identity as a result of the encounter with the other who is "flesh of his flesh."

sexual passion or sunbathing, but in the world of the Bible it expresses rather the state of being unprotected and hence potentially vulnerable. Nakedness without shame is the condition of small children, and denotes a lack of self-consciousness which enables one to be seen as one is. It is the state of an innocence which is not (yet) wounded. The first couple is thus presented as living in an unreflective trust, with no need to conceal or protect their weaker parts. As the narrative will go on to show, this naïve innocence is both a great gift, since it makes possible openness to the other and therefore relationship, and eminently fragile, easily susceptible of being subverted. Its ambivalent quality expresses the uniquely "unfinished" character of human existence: *homo sapiens* is the only species on the road to something greater, and continually placed before alternatives on the way to becoming who it is ultimately meant to be.

The Wisdom of the Serpent

But before the drama or intrigue properly speaking can begin, another player must appear on the stage. That player is the snake. Here we have another example of how hard it is to read a well-known text as given, without projecting upon it our preconceptions. Very quickly in the Judeo-Christian tradition, and undoubtedly because of this story, the snake became a personification of evil. This tendency exists already in the New Testament. The Book of Revelation speaks of *the great Dragon* which is *the ancient Serpent, called the Devil and Satan, the deceiver of the whole world* (Revelation 12:9). It is important to realize that such an identification is a **consequence** of meditating upon this story, and not a prior given. If we take the narrative as it is, the snake is simply... a snake. Not a snake as we know it, to be sure, since, among other things, this one speaks. It is not, however, identified explicitly with the demonic, but simply referred to as one of the *living things of the fields*, in other words an undomesticated animal.

The snake is further qualified as the most 'arum of all the animals. Here, our author engages in another bit of characteristic wordplay. In the previous verse, the man and woman were described as 'arumim, naked, the plural of 'arom. The snake, however, is not naked but "astute, clever"; the word, often translated in this context as "crafty" or "cunning," does not in fact have negative connotations in itself. In the Book of Proverbs, the 'arum is viewed with approval. Such an individual is often contrasted with the *pethi*, the "simple person," a word which can also occasionally be positive but which generally has the connotation of one who is young and inexperienced, and thus easily seduced:

> The *pethi* believes everything
> but the 'arum watches his step.
> (Proverbs 14:15; cf. 14:18; 22:3)

The narrative thus clearly places us once again in a context of reflection on wisdom, with the opposition between the "simple" and the "clever" expressing itself in the dialogue between the naked ('arom) woman and the shrewd ('arum) serpent. This bit of wordplay is enough to show that the narrative itself is not so "simple" and straightforward as it might appear, but is quite a sophisticated reflection on what it means to be human.

Let us consider the symbolism of the snake a moment longer. Outside of Israel, as we have seen, figures of animals were commonly used to symbolize the supernatural world. The serpent was one of these figures. In many civilizations it stood for wisdom. An earth-symbol par excellence, the snake was sometimes associated with regeneration, presumably because of its ability to shed its skin. In Canaan and elsewhere, it was thus apparently linked to the cult of fertility. In Greek mythology, it represented healing and was found on the staff of the god Asclepius, which is used still today as a symbol for the medical profession. Surprisingly, the serpent as a divine image was venerated for a long time in Israel as well, despite the official ban on idols. In the Exodus story we find an attempt to explain — or to explain away — this custom:

> The Lord sent fiery serpents among the people and they bit the people and many of the Israelites died. The people went to Moses and said, "We have sinned because we have spoken against the Lord and against you. Intercede to the Lord to take away the snakes from us." So Moses interceded on behalf of the people. And the Lord said to Moses, "Make for yourself a fiery serpent and put it on a pole. And all those who were bitten and look upon it will live." So Moses made a bronze snake and put it on a pole and if a snake bit someone, that person would look at the bronze snake and would live.   (Numbers 21:6-9)

Many centuries later, we read about the reformer-king Hezekiah:

> He cut down the sacred pole and shattered to bits the bronze snake that Moses made, because up till that time the children of Israel were offering incense-sacrifices to it. It was called Nehushtan.   (2 Kings 18:4)

It may astonish us that Jesus, for his part, does not hesitate to compare himself to this serpent:

> Just as Moses raised up a serpent in the wilderness, so the
> Son of man must be raised up, so that whoever believes
> in him will have eternal life.   (John 3:14-15)

And he identifies the snake as a symbol of wisdom, encouraging his disciples to imitate it. Jesus does not see cleverness as opposed to simplicity; in his mind, a disciple is called to reconcile what is best in the two approaches to reality.

> Be judicious like serpents and innocent like doves.
>   (Matthew 10:16)

In short, those who see the serpent exclusively as an image of evil would do well first to consider the roots of the symbol in the world of wisdom. In the narrative of Genesis 2–3, concerned as it is with the question of true wisdom, it certainly functions in this way.

This being said, we must add at once that all wisdom is not identical. What kind of practical intelligence does the snake represent in our story? Are there different kinds of wisdom? A New Testament book, the Letter of James, replies in the affirmative:

> This is not the wisdom come down from above but
> an earthly, unspiritual, demonic sort. (...) The wisdom
> from above, on the other hand, is first of all innocent,
> then peace-loving, good-natured, willing to listen, full
> of mercy and the fruits of goodness, free from prejudice
> and hypocrisy.   (James 3:15-17)

James' reflection is very close to what our narrative is attempting to depict. If, in order to attain the good life, human beings must inevitably seek and find an answer to the question, "How should we live?" — which in biblical terms is the question of wisdom, then the essential question posed by the human condition can be rephrased in the following way: "In what does true wisdom consist?"

The story has already proposed one implicit response to this question. True wisdom consists in listening to the voice of God, who knows better than we do what authentic life entails. It thus means recognizing our limits — understanding that we are not the source of life — and receiving everything we are and have as a gift of divine generosity. Within this universe-as-gift, there is plenty of room for the exercise of human freedom and intelligence. The earthling has to use his gifts to care for the garden in which God has placed him. And as farmers have always known, the work of cultivating plants and breeding animals requires a great deal of practical know-how, a feel for the rhythms of the seasons and knowledge of the things of the earth. To understand the story correctly, it should be clear that the exercise of intelligence is in no way excluded from the good life desired by God. The ideal human being in God's eyes is neither a child nor a fool.

But this "wisdom of the earth," so necessary for human existence, has its own proper place; left to itself, it tends to occupy center stage and to become the sole criterion for making choices. When human life is not worked out in collaboration with the divine Source but rather is entwined around itself like a snake, in a solipsistic fascination with its own powers, then it eventually destroys the very ground on which it is standing. In the language of Genesis 3, when the earthling enters into a dialogue not with God but with the snake, then all of life is perverted.

This distinction between divine and earthly wisdom — the wisdom of God and the wisdom of the serpent — can be summed up in the two words "religion" and "magic." A modern rationalistic mentality often equates the two, whereas in fact they are diametrically opposed. Religion consists essentially in the recognition of a higher power to which human beings owe reverence and even submission. Magic is the attempt by humans to appropriate the laws of the universe for their own ends, whether good or evil ones: there is both "white" and "black" magic. The serpent is a manifest symbol of magic, which is one of the reasons why it was abhorred by pious believers in Israel. But it needs to be emphasized that not all magic is to be proscribed. Once again, human beings need to become familiar with the laws that govern the universe in order to gain some mastery over their environment and thus fulfill their God-given calling to take care of the earth. Modern science and technology is essentially a magical enterprise. And if I need bypass surgery on my heart, I want a surgeon who not only prays and believes in a higher power but one who knows his business, who has received good training and exercised his talents. In the same way, if I have to fly across the ocean, I hope that the engineers who designed and built the aircraft were diligent students and take their work seriously. Nevertheless, magic by its nature tends to compete with and ultimately eclipse religion. Our contemporary Western civilization is a dramatic example of this. With all of our practical know-how, is not our lack of true wisdom leading us to the brink of the abyss? The questions posed by Genesis 2-3 would seem to be more relevant than ever for our world today.

Duel to the Death

The next scene in our narrative is a dialogue between the snake and the earthling, represented by the woman. It is a small masterpiece of composition: in true reptilian fashion, the serpent worms its way into the relationship between the humans and their God, effectively demolishing the trust that makes any relationship possible. In her innocence and lack of experience, the woman is no match for the wiles of the worldly-wise snake.

Before examining the dialogue more closely, we must deal with a prior question which has provided the misogynist reading of the text with some of its strongest ammunition. On the surface, it appears curious that the privileged conversational partner of the snake is the woman. Why does the serpent speak only with her?

The prevailing answer to this question down through the ages has been the following one: because females are the weaker sex. Therefore, goes the argument, the adversary follows a tried-and-true strategy by attacking his opponent's weakest point.

Those who hold to this interpretation, however, have often cast doubt upon it by a manifest contradiction in their own reasoning. Women are weak, gullible, unable to reason, goes the litany, but they are also born seducers and manipulators, supremely capable of bending (weaker) men to their will. Since the text itself provides no information to back up this reading, it simply functions as a blank slate upon which can be projected all the grievances certain males have accumulated against the opposite sex.

Is there any objective data in the story itself which could help us to understand why the snake converses with the woman? One particularity lies in the fact that the woman is a late arrival on the scene. The earthling had received the commandment directly from the Lord when the woman was not yet present. She is thus in the same situation as the hearers of the story, who have presumably not received any direct communication from God but have come into contact with the divine Word through other human beings — or by reading Scripture, which comes in the end to the same thing. The woman here is thus a better model for us in our attempt to be faithful to God, since neither she nor we benefit from a direct revelation.[21]

A second possibility concerns the woman's specific role in the story. In this regard, it is significant that most people, notably those who defend the misogynic reading, assume that the snake has surprised the woman while she is alone, all the better to deceive her. Her partner is presumably off somewhere busy with his own masculine pastimes. In fact, as v. 6 tells us explicitly, the man is *with her.* So then the question is not just why the snake addresses the woman, but why the man lets her do all the talking! After a pause for the inevitable jests, we may conjecture that the real reason has to do with her God-given role in the community of two. She is the *ezer,* the help.

Although the word *ezer* refers to help in a general sense, there is one particular kind of helper found later on in Scripture that may shed light on our question. Before leaving his disciples to return to the Father, Jesus tells them that he will not leave them alone but will ask the Father to send them *another Paraclete* to be with them for ever (John 14:16). The word *parakletos,* in Latin *advocatus,* literally means "someone called beside" to

---

[21] I am indebted for this suggestion to the book of André Wénin, *Actualité des mythes: Relire les récits mythiques de Genèse 1–11* (Namur: Centre de Formation Cardijn, décembre 1997), p. 31-32.

give help, support or encouragement. In the realm of the law, it refers to the advocate or attorney who stands before the judge and speaks in another's name. In the First Letter of John, Jesus himself is presented as the Paraclete who defends us before the Father (1 John 2:1). Is it not therefore appropriate for the *isshah*, who comes from the side of *ha-adam* and then stands at his side, to exercise her role as helper by speaking in the name of them both? In her, the word comes to its full flowering. She would consequently be addressed not because she is the weaker link, but because she is the one called in this situation to wage the combat for humanity against the enemies of life. In defeating her, the snake will have achieved a total victory.

Although she is the best that humankind has to offer at the moment, the woman is clearly out of her depth when trying to deal with this kind of conversational partner. Instead of using outright lies, relatively easy to counter, the snake subtly twists God's words and makes them say the opposite of what they originally meant. He thus gradually leads the woman to a vision of God which is diametrically opposed to the reality, without her even realizing that she has been tricked. This story shows beyond a doubt that all forms of reasoning are not equal. It is not the capacity to reason which is at fault; reason can serve different ends according to the spirit which lies behind it. This assertion is not of theoretical interest alone, because the reasoning of the serpent is very much alive and well in our contemporary world.

The very first words spoken by the snake set the scene and ensure his control over the situation. *So, did God really say...?* From the start the snake establishes an illusory complicity with his conversational partner: no introduction needs to be made or original distance overcome; he simply speaks to her as if they were old friends. One can almost see him whispering snake-like in her ear, to such an extent that the voice seems to come from within her. And as a matter of fact, the biblical author may well be trying to evoke not so much a true interpersonal dialogue as an inner debate. A snake, after all, is not an appropriate partner for the earthling (cf. Genesis 2:20). By treating it as such, the woman makes her first mistake. In this regard the prayer of Saint Augustine comes to mind: "O Truth, Light of my heart, do not let my darkness speak to me" (*Confessions* XII, 10, 10). This is precisely what the woman fails to do.

The snake thus begins by asking a question. On the surface this appears to be an innocent undertaking; one asks in order to discover what one does not know. But the turn of phrase used betrays an underlying doubt: *af ki amar... So, did God really say...?* And the statement attributed to God, while not strictly speaking false, subtly changes the import of his words: *You shall not eat from all the trees in the garden.* The words as given are ambiguous, since they could mean "You may not eat from **any** of the trees in the garden" (not all = none) or "There are **some** trees from which you may not eat" (not all = some). The first proposition is clearly false, while the second, although literally true, contradicts the tenor of God's words. It places the accent on what is forbidden, whereas God emphasized in the first place the earthlings' positive freedom to enjoy the fruits of the garden, except for the limit case, the tree in the center, necessary to make the rest possible. By thus focusing on the limit, the snake's words transform the image of God from that of a Giver of life to someone who withholds it, and indeed implicitly accuse God of being a liar.[22]

---

[22] Compare 2:16: *You (sing.) shall freely eat of all the trees of the garden* and 3:1: *You (pl.) shall not eat of all the trees of the garden.*

Right from the outset, the woman is thus placed in an impossible position. There are ways of asking questions that are
in themselves a trap, since to give any answer one must already
enter into the biased outlook of the questioner, and any reply
is therefore compromising. In such cases the only authentic response is to refuse to engage in the dialogue as defined by the
questioner — either to subvert the presuppositions or to remain
silent.[23] But the woman is inexperienced, so she simply takes
the snake's question at face value and does her best to reply. She
corrects what she considers a wrong interpretation, namely that
all the trees are forbidden, and then repeats God's command.
But in so doing she makes it more extreme: on her lips what
is forbidden is not only to eat from the tree at the center of the
garden, but even to touch it. Like a child (as has already been
mentioned, this story becomes most comprehensible when the
man and woman are viewed as innocent children), she does
not really understand what she is commanded to do and not to
do. All she can do is to parrot back the words she has received,
which are then subtly deformed because they are not set in the
right context. Detached from the underlying intention, the prohibition takes on a life of its own and is therefore exaggerated.

Now the serpent goes on the attack. He flatly contradicts
God's words while again distorting their meaning. What was a
warning about the inevitable consequences of the act is implicitly
treated as a threat, still worse an empty threat. He paints the
portrait of a God jealous of his prerogatives, not wanting to share
his life with his creatures. Whereas the previous chapter depicted
a Creator God whose fundamental desire was to communicate

---

[23] In the Gospels we find Jesus using both of these tactics, calling into question
the presuppositions of the questioner (see e.g. Matthew 21:24; 22:15-22; Luke
10:29-37) and remaining silent (Mark 14:61; John 8:6).

life to humanity and call it to share in the task of nurturing the universe, the "God" presented by the snake is a sadistic being who wishes to prevent humans from being "like God" at all costs. The snake's deception goes even further, for his words assume that what makes God God is the ability "to know good and evil." While this is accurate in the sense that only God possesses true wisdom, it is not true in the sense intended by the snake, namely, that God can do whatever he wants. This kind of false view of divine omnipotence, it should be noted, still keeps many people from believing in the God of the Bible. God's power does not consist in being able to act as arbitrarily as possible, to be "a law unto himself." God is almighty because he is always fully who he is, fully true to his identity. And if God is love, as Saint John tells us, then all God can do is love. Speaking of God's power is a way of asserting that divine love is efficacious; God acts in perfect harmony with his wisdom and his justice, and his acts infallibly achieve their ends (cf. Isaiah 55:10-11).

A Before and an After

The snake's devious reasoning has succeeded in its intent, so he can now depart from the scene. It has sown doubt in the woman concerning the identity of the Creator, and has therefore made a breach in the implicit trust that linked the two together. No longer enveloped in this mutual trust, the woman's fundamental way of relating to the world is altered radically. When we turn our backs on the source of wisdom, refusing to listen to the words of the One who knows best the truth of existence, then all that remains is personal experience. The woman now "looks": she has become an empiricist.

And what does she see? That the tree is capable of satisfying different longings in her: the need for food (though she could eat from many other trees, ones that are not forbidden) and, deeper still, for insight. Through the words of God reinforced and deformed by the snake, she has realized that there is a link between this tree and the acquisition of wisdom. In this regard it is perhaps not by chance that the verb *sakal,* which can be translated "to have insight," also means "to be successful." Her desire for wisdom is not disinterested.

In addition, between the longing for food and for insight, the woman observes that the tree is *desirable to the eyes.* While the contemplation of beauty and its attractive power are not blameworthy in themselves, in this context the beautiful object serves as a magnet to draw out and bind her desire. In short, if the woman is an empiricist, she is not a wholly successful one, because her observation is not detached. It is at the service of a desire which is naively self-interested. When this desire which characterizes human beings does not undergo the necessary transformations in its quest for an object truly capable of satisfying it, then it can indeed be seen as at the source of all evil.[24]

The most insightful comment on this verse of Genesis comes, perhaps surprisingly, from a New Testament book, the First Letter of John. Speaking of what he calls *the love of the world,* which in his language means an enthrallment with human and social realities as an end in themselves, the author writes:

---

[24] It cannot be emphasized enough that the Bible does not condemn desire in itself, but rather a desire which stops short before reaching its true goal. For a fuller discussion see Brother John of Taizé, *Reading the Ten Commandments Anew: Towards a Land of Freedom* (New York: ST PAULS/Alba House, 2004), p. 111-117.

All that is in the world — the desire of the flesh and the
desire of the eyes and pride in material things — is not
from the Father but from the world. Now the world and
its desire is passing away, but whoever does the will of
God remains for ever.   (1 John 2:16-17)

What is wrong with this desire is that it mistakenly attaches
itself to what is not worthy of it; it causes us to cling to realities destined to perish. That is the mistake which the woman is
about to make.

She took of the fruit and ate. After the long preparation
necessary to get to this point, the act itself is quite simple, ap-
pearing almost trivial. Yet because of it everything changes; there
is a before and an after in the narrative. An irrevocable step has
been taken, with enormous and incalculable consequences for all
that will follow. In this story we see the full ontological density
of human action quite dramatically portrayed: as collaborators
in the ongoing divine work of creation, human beings have the
power by their acts to create a more hospitable world or one
which is ultimately self-destructive. Even apparently insignificant
acts either contribute to making the universe better or have the
opposite effect. In this case, the entire destiny of the world turns
on the simple act of eating some fruit.

Before going on, we would do well to emphasize once
again the significance in this story of the act of "taking and eating
the fruit of the tree of the knowledge of good and evil," since
this is of vital importance for understanding the true meaning
of Genesis 3. It does not mean simply "wishing to tell right from
wrong" or, in other words, wanting to have the wisdom necessary
to lead a good life. As already stated, if this tree is at the center
of the garden, to the point where it is practically indistinguishable
from the tree of life, this means that for human beings the

knowledge it offers is of the utmost importance in order to live a fully human life. The search for wisdom is an indispensable part of the human project, indeed the most essential part of all, and it is absurd to imagine that the divine commandment intends to curtail this search. That is what the serpent wants us to believe and, in a word, it is a lie. The story in fact turns round the further question of "**How** do we achieve true wisdom?" and presents an alternative: either by trusting in God and therefore paying attention to his Word, which also means accepting our need to trust, and therefore our limits; or else refusing to trust and viewing our limits as obstacles to attaining the fullness of life. The woman's act expresses her implicit choice of the second road, the will to appropriate for herself the source of life and the knowledge about how to live, to see them as possessions and not as gifts to be gratefully received and developed.[25]

By expressing this in story form and not discursively, the text allows us to participate in the same drama as the couple in the garden. As the many interpretations show, the text remains open; we are free to accept the wisdom of the snake, in whole or in part, rather than to listen to the voice of God. Since the consequences of this alternative are not immediately perceptible, we may well believe the snake's contention that by taking the forbidden fruit we will not die, that this warning is merely a ruse to safeguard God's privileges and to keep us from enjoying true happiness. While each of us is called to make the choice for his

---

[25] It is striking that, in 1 Kings 3:5-15, we have a story of how the young king Solomon, when offered any possible gift by God, asked for *an understanding heart to govern..., able to discern between good and evil* (v. 9). If Genesis 2–3 was composed during or shortly after the reign of Solomon, or is at any rate contemporary with this story, then each sheds light on the other. In the mind of the inspired author of the Book of Kings, Solomon found true wisdom because he asked for and received it from the Lord.

or her own part, our world is likewise engaged in a long-term experiment to test the truth of these claims. In this sense, this age-old story remains more relevant than ever.

A Chain of Consequences

Following the woman's act, everything falls to pieces. The narrative shows the consequences that follow one after another, like the ripples of a pebble thrown into a pond. First of all, *she also gave [the fruit] to her* ish *with her, and he ate.* The unity of the couple, that great gift of being two-in-one-flesh as a result of God's act, now entails that the wrong choice of one will contaminate the other; the supreme good of human community is perverted. And how much damage does not solidarity in wrong-doing still do today?

It is interesting that the man is depicted here as totally passive; he puts up no resistance but merely takes and eats what is handed to him. The misogynist reading of the text not-withstanding, the woman does not need to seduce her partner, to overcome his resistance; there is no resistance and therefore no seduction. This confirms the interpretation offered in these pages of the woman's role as the "paraclete," the advocate or defender who speaks for them both. Once she has given way, the dike has broken and both are swept away in the flood. They are "one flesh" for better and for worse.

The next consequence of the act is a highly ironic one: *And the eyes of both were opened....* The snake's prediction seems to have come true, since the couple has now acquired greater insight. But what in fact do they see? That they are naked! Bereft of divine protection, they see themselves as they are without God — limited and vulnerable. Wishing to be like God, they discover that as "gods," in other words beings who are self-sufficient, they are sadly lacking. Here the narrative borrows a motif that enjoys great success in traditional tales: after finally having their deepest wishes granted by the gods, human beings find that the result is the opposite of what they had foreseen, a source of affliction and not of joy. This motif reveals a profound truth of the human condition, and one that is at the center of Genesis 2-3: left to our own devices, we do not know what we truly want; the road to true life is not what we imagine it to be.

The negative consequences of their new self-knowledge are shown above all by the need to hide. This means first of all to hide from themselves and from each other, and that is what we call **shame**. Returning to the theme of nakedness, the text registers a significant difference. Earlier they were not ashamed, but now they notice their nakedness and make loincloths for themselves. Clothing here is not presented as protection against inclement weather but against the eyes of the other, implying that the wearer finds his or her vulnerability intolerable and re-gards the other as a threat. In this regard we should mention a rabbinical explanation of why the man and the woman did not feel ashamed before eating the forbidden fruit. It was because they were clothed in God's glory, in other words in garments of light. To clothe one's nakedness is not an irrational act, but it was not necessary earlier, since trust in God served as their shield. Now that this trust is gone, they have to replace it by makeshift substitutes. Making an article of clothing is the first specifically cultural act in the story, and one which requires practical know-how. Is it going too far to say that the narrative thus presents human culture as the attempt to remedy our fun-damental nakedness, to mitigate the loss of direct communion with God by artifacts of our own design?

We should mention in passing that, here as in general, bodily shame focuses above all on the reproductive and excretory organs. Certain interpretations of Genesis 3 notwithstanding, the story does not deal primarily with sexuality. If the human need to hide and protect the most intimate self is symbolized by that part of the body that is concerned with interpersonal communion and the generation of new life on the one hand, and the elimination of waste matter on the other, that cannot be an accident. Is it not there that the contrast and possible confusion become most acute between our limited nature and our God-given vocation, between the animal and the divine of which our body is the point of encounter?

After hiding from themselves and each other, the next step is to hide from God. Here the narrative takes a surprisingly archaic turn, depicting God in a highly anthropomorphic guise, a bit like a gentleman in Victorian England taking a turn in his garden to benefit from the evening breeze. In fact, what we probably have here is a reminiscence of the myths prevalent in the ancient Middle East concerning the garden of the gods. On a quite different level, we are reminded again of the behavior of small children. Mother has forbidden them to touch the cookie jar while she is away; they disobey her and, in so doing, break the jar. When they hear the sound of her key in the lock, they run away and hide under the bed. It is just as rational to attempt to hide from God as it is for children to hide from their parents; far from saving them, their flight is already a clear sign that they have done something wrong. And yet the impulse to run and hide in such cases is imperious. In a kind of vicious circle, sin causes us to place distance between ourselves and God, which paradoxically cuts us off from the only true source of healing.

And just like a parent, God knows immediately what has

happened. He nonetheless pursues the wayward children and questions them to elicit the story. God calls out to the earthling; his first words are *Where are you?* What better way to emphasize that the God of the Bible is a God who calls, who keeps on inviting us to a relationship with himself, even when we are attempting to hide from his face? If God agrees to play hide-and-seek with us in this way, is it not because he knows that only in communion with him can we find the fullness of life which we are constantly seeking in all of our waywardness?

Establishing the Truth

The next scene in the story has two parts. God first questions the man and the woman to establish the truth of what happened and then makes decisions based upon this investigation. Although the best way to understand the text is to imagine a parent with her disobedient children, the author in fact employs the categories of a trial in court: the judge must first ascertain the offense by interrogating the parties involved and then render a verdict. Again, God's questions are not so much to inform him of what happened as to reveal the implicit motivations for the culprits' behavior and to get them to acknowledge their wrong-doing. By bringing to light what was hidden, the questioning offers the guilty parties a road to healing, since forgiveness involves admitting one's complicity with evil and in this way separating it from one's authentic self.

The man's first response shows clearly that something has changed. Implicit trust has given way to fear. This is not "fear of the Lord" in the positive sense of the term, but precisely the opposite. That kind of "fear" means in reality recognizing God as God, and in fact it is *the beginning of wisdom,* as the Bible never tires of repeating (Proverbs 9:10; cf. 1:7; 15:33; Psalm 111:10; Job 28:28; Sirach 1:14, 20). Here, it was a fear of being harmed which had caused the man to run away. Like a good investigator, God immediately puts his finger on what has changed, and points to the certain cause, albeit as a question: *Have you eaten of the tree…?*

To the extent that this dialogue offers a potential opportunity for healing through the recognition of truth, the following two replies are highly disappointing. Instead of admitting to the obvious fact of his guilt, the man projects the blame on his companion. In fact he goes even further, implicitly casting the blame upon God: *The woman whom* **you gave** *to be with me,* **she gave** *me fruit….* God's gift is thus perversely seen merely as an excuse to abdicate responsibility. For her part the woman blames the snake for deceiving her, thus implicitly revealing her lack of wisdom. And since the snake is not a being able to enter into a personal relationship with God, this is equivalent to saying that nobody is guilty of the crime. (It should be noted that God does not ask the snake any questions, and indeed the snake has remained mute ever since the woman took the fruit.)[26]

With a great deal of psychological astuteness, the biblical narrator describes a fundamental "law" of evil: it has as a corollary the refusal to assume responsibility. "No-man" did it. In this way, too, wrongdoing runs away from the light and hides.

---

[26] Here the later identification between the snake and personified evil finds a justification as well as a limit. God cannot enter into a direct dialogue with evil, because it has no personal existence as such. It manifests itself only obliquely, when persons attribute ultimate significance to what is not absolute. Evil is by its very nature a corner-of-the-eye or a behind-the-back phenomenon. When one attempts to face it directly it vanishes or loses its hold, since it has no face but is expressed only in a game of masks.

We blame others for our missteps or, better still, we blame the snake, in other words the non-human world of causality seen as determining our behavior: "It was my upbringing, my social class, my psychological problems, etc., that made me do it." Blaming the snake is naturally preferable to blaming others, since the snake cannot talk back. When, however, we take responsibility for our mistakes, we have already taken a step beyond them. We are on the road to discovering our full humanity in a relationship with the God who wants no one to die, but encourages them to return to him and live (cf. Ezekiel 33:11).

In addition, the refusal to take responsibility and the projection of our own evil on others effectively destroys the mutual solidarity that is the basis of all life in society. Individuals and societies have used projection for ages to shore up their own identity at the cost of distancing themselves from others. The cohesion of the group is reinforced by finding and isolating a scapegoat who is seen as bearing responsibility for all of society's ills: the Jews, the blacks, the Communists, the Christians.... Paradoxically, unity is achieved against or at the expense of others. An identity based on projection is evidently a fragile one, since it requires the denial of the full humanity of the other and thus of one's own full humanity: what we reject in the other is for the most part what we refuse at all costs to see in ourselves. Characteristically, this fragility is compensated for by the violence with which the projection is maintained, and its long-term result is the breakup of the human community. In Genesis 3, the inspired author shows this process in embryo, with all of its devastating potential.

In just a few lines, then, the narrative shows the chain of consequences that follow from refusing to listen to the voice of God and to recognize one's limits: hiding from oneself and from others; running away from the Source, now viewed as inimical to true life; and finally, the destruction of human community by scapegoating the other. God had earlier predicted that breaking the relationship of trust in him would lead to death (cf. Genesis 2:17), and this prediction is now well on its way to being fulfilled.

The Divine Verdict

Once the judge has completed the investigation, it is time for the verdict to be rendered and the sentence carried out. Or, in the case of a parent, the appropriate discipline needs to be found. The old word for this was punishment, and as we would expect after centuries marked by a moralistic reading of the Bible, this is the way most people read this part of the story, as an account of God punishing sinful humanity. Unfortunately, this reading merely reinforces a view already far too widespread, that of the God of the Bible — or at least of the Old Testament — as a harsh and even vindictive disciplinarian, eager to find and penalize the smallest infraction of his arbitrary laws. The fact that such a vision of the deity has little to do with the true message of Scripture does not keep it from being found everywhere. It is therefore crucial to look more closely at the text to see what in fact is going on.

The best way to understand what "punishment" could mean in this context is, once again, to take the example of loving parents whose children have done something potentially dangerous that they have already been warned against. Let us assume that they have left the yard and have been found playing out in the street. The main concern of the parents is naturally how to prevent such behavior in the future, and to do so if possible not by outward constraints such as building a fence around the yard, but by helping the children grasp the danger. The goal of such "punishment" is twofold. First of all, it should allow the culprits to taste the harmful consequences of the act they have performed. Often, as in our hypothetical example, it is almost impossible to do this directly, so some other unpleasant but less extreme experience must be substituted. When possible, however, the best method is to let the wrongdoers experience directly the adverse consequences of their chosen behavior, so that they will not repeat it in the future.

At the same time — and this is the second aspect of disciplinary activity on the part of teachers anxious that the lesson be learned — the penalty must not be so severe that it harms the culprit or eliminates all desire to behave differently. In other words, there must be a dimension of **promise** hidden within it, so that all hope is not lost. The carrot must be joined to the stick. These two aspects merge in the image of "bitter medicine," which is why this is so often used as a metaphor for what we are attempting to describe. It is never pleasant to take such medicine, but if used properly it leads to true health and ultimately becomes unnecessary.

Since the story we are examining appears to have deep roots in the soil of Wisdom literature, it is not surprising that God is presented here as a wise judge or educator. In fact, his judgments are ideal examples of true discipline with its two dimensions of deterrence and promise. This means in addition that, for the inspired author of this narrative, human life as we know it — as opposed to the way God originally intended it — is primarily a process of learning "the hard way." It inevitably involves an encounter with painful resistances that, at least potentially, can prepare us one day to receive authentic life.

Let us now look at the divine verdicts more closely. First of all, God curses the snake. A curse in the Bible is a legal procedure for the removal of a blessing, in other words of a gift of life, and it is dramatized in the following words by the injunction to crawl on the ground and eat dust. If we remember that in Genesis 2:7 the first living being was created from the dust, and also recall that in the world of the Bible bronze serpents were put up on poles and seen as the manifestation of a certain kind of wisdom, it is easy to understand that what we have here is the opposite movement, a kind of de-creation which takes the form of a demotion. Since the snake has no personal identity, what God is condemning here is not the reptile itself but what it represents. In other words, God formally declares that what we have called "the wisdom of the serpent" is not the road to true life. For Israel this implied the refusal of magic, whereby humans attempt to take charge of the universe according to their own lights.

We should note that the snake is not put to death, however, but merely brought to the ground. The idol is pulled off its pedestal (cf. 2 Kings 18:4). It is thus subordinated to the human beings, and in the following verse their relationship is described as one of conflict. In the language of the story, then, what the snake represents is not totally proscribed; it must rather be subservient to the human and, even more so, to the divine. In other words, the kind of wisdom it stands for has a role to play in the relationship between human beings and the material world, but a clearly subordinate one. When allowed to gain the upper hand, it becomes demonic. We can define a demon as a created reality that has usurped the place of God. When humans become enamored of the works of their hands to such an extent that efficiency, technical progress and success at all costs become the sole or ultimate criteria for their choices, then they are in thrall to the wisdom of the serpent. Is not the conflict between the woman, who represents what is human, and the snake more relevant than ever in the world today, where the technological resources offered by modern science open up mind-boggling possibilities? Someone has expressed our contemporary dilemma well by saying: in a world where we **can** now do almost everything we want, what **should** we do? According to Genesis 3, this question cannot be answered on the basis of scientific or narrowly rational calculations alone. An answer which is authentically human requires a wisdom that can only come from an openness to, and a trust in, the supra-human Ground of our being.

Let us pause a moment to look more closely at v. 15. We have seen that true correction involves, in addition to tasting the unpleasant consequences of one's behavior, glimpsing the promise of a positive outcome. This verse presents the first expression of that hope. For that reason, certain early Christians referred to it as the *protoevangelion*, the "first good news." It predicts that the conflict between what the snake represents and what the woman represents will go on throughout history, and there is a nuanced affirmation that in the end *the offspring of the woman* will conquer. Taking this expression in a singular and masculine sense turn these words into a prophecy of the coming of the Messiah, and establish a link between the Woman of Genesis 2-3 and Mary, the mother of the Lord. In any event, we have here the first mention of *offspring* (seed) and thus of life that continues. This clearly implies that, in God's eyes, the threat of death for humankind is not an immediate or necessarily a definitive one.

Childbearing and Hard Labor

God now turns to the woman, and continues the mention of children. The verb "to multiply," which is generally used in connection with the divine blessing and refers to the propagation of life through descendants (cf. Genesis 1:22, 28; 8:17; 9:1 etc.), is now employed in the context of procreation but, paradoxically, with *pain* as its object:

> I will greatly multiply your travail in childbearing. In pain
> you will give birth to children.   (Genesis 3:16a)

Promise and difficulty are again inseparably wedded. The fact that life will continue is good news, but this will not happen without suffering. The story thus invites us to take an empirical fact, namely that childbirth is a painful process, as a symbol recapitulating the human condition. The road to the fullness of life is not something automatic or easy, but involves a sometimes painful break with the acquisitions to which we tend to cling.

The second part of this verse is more enigmatic, and has consequently been interpreted in different ways:

> Your desire will be for your *ish*, and he will rule over
> you.   (Genesis 3:16b)

What is clear at any rate is that because of what has happened, the relationship between the *ish* and the *isshah* has been modified. It has become asymmetrical. Commentators differ on the significance of this verse insofar as the verb "to rule over, master," can have either positive or negative connotations.[27] If the mastery is seen as positive, it could be a way of saying that

---

[27] This is not, incidentally, the same verb as the one found in Genesis 1:26, 28. It is used rather in Genesis 1:16 to speak of the sun and the moon.

desire (here associated with the *isshah*) must in the future be
subordinated to authentically human criteria (here represented
by *adam* insofar as he received from God the call to watch
over creation in God's name, cf. Genesis 1:26; 2:15). Analogous
to the way the wisdom of the snake must be judged in function of a higher purpose, so too human desire cannot become
an end in itself. Although this reading of the text offends our
contemporary sensibilities, because the woman symbolizes the
part of humanity that needs to be subordinated, it would only
be a misogynist interpretation strictly speaking if "desire" were
seen as something reprehensible, and there is no suggestion in
the phrase that this is the case.[28]

In the second creation story, however, the mission which
was given to the earthling by God was not defined in terms of
ruling or having dominion, which would seem to imply that this
kind of relationship between the sexes is not part of the original
intention of the Creator. At best it is a stopgap solution, one that
does not express the deepest and truest meaning of the conjugal
bond. Whereas at the moment of her creation the *isshah* was
defined by the *ish* as *bone of my bones and flesh of my flesh* (2:
23), now we have the asymmetrical relationship of desiring/
ruling. Domination and subordination seem to have taken the
place of mutuality. If the couple is taken as the prototype of all
human relationships, the text suggests that in the new dispensa-
tion, in a world marked by the refusal to trust, human beings
will certainly still need each other (cf. 2:18), but that this desire
for fellowship will not easily lead to relationships of true equality and reciprocity. It confirms the truth of the observation that,

---

[28] An argument in favor of reading the verb "to dominate" as positive is given by
the fact that the very same construction is used in Genesis 4:7, *its desire is for
you, but you will rule over it*. In chapter 4, however, *sin*, not a human being, is
the subject of the phrase.

in a world where God is not taken into account, we are trapped on the horns of a dilemma — we cannot get along without one another and yet we cannot get along with each other either.

Now it is the man's turn. His partner's sentence had to do with childbirth, and now his concerns work. First of all, because of his act the soil loses its blessing, which in this case means fertility, the capacity to sustain life. *Adam* came from *adamah*, and now, by a reverse movement, the *adamah* suffers the consequences of the sin of the *adam*. The Book of Genesis illustrates once again the deep bonds linking humanity and the rest of creation, bonds which in our day have been brought to light on a somewhat different basis by the ecological movement. That outlook, incidentally, shares with Genesis the conviction that to bring back our planet to a healthy condition, human beings must alter their habits, their way of life. The wisdom of the serpent promotes an unbridled manipulation and exploitation of nature, with human desire as the only criterion. It leads to the loss of the original blessing, transforming a beautiful garden into a barren waste.

Because of this new situation, the earthling and the earth are henceforth not a partnership but exist in a relationship of mutual hostility. Humans must extract their food from the earth through harsh labor. Work, which in the first part of the story was presented as a gratifying collaboration with the activity of the Creator, is now seen by its other face — that of hard and unrewarding toil. Life goes on, and in this sense the blessing has not entirely disappeared, but God's final words seem categorical:

> By the sweat of your face you shall eat bread until you return to the ground (*adamah*), for out of it you were taken. For you are dust, and to dust you shall return.
>
> (Genesis 3:19)

Detached from the divine will and the divine promise, the only outlook for humankind is death. Once again this is presented as a kind of de-creation, a reverse movement by which we return to the starting-point (cf. Psalm 104:29-30). If what enabled a living being to come into existence was the breath of God which transformed the dust of the earth into something radically different (see Genesis 2:7), then it stands to reason that when the link with God is broken, human beings sink back into their component parts. They have no independent existence; they are not in themselves the Source and cannot hold themselves in being. The story thus shows with great perspicacity the folly of humans' imagining that they can simply work out their own existence by following their own self-chosen ends and means. When they try to play God in this way, they saw off the very branch on which they are sitting and place their very existence in peril. The true meaning of God's first words to the earthling is spelled out (cf. 2:17): the only horizon of a self-centered existence is death.

Were these the last words of the story, the perspective would indeed be bleak, not to say hopeless. But the fact that life will go on, albeit with difficulty, shows that even here there is a hope hidden within the divine verdict. In the final judgment of the man, the immediate death that God's words earlier seemed to indicate is nuanced (compare 2:17b *on the day* and 3:17 *all the days of your life*). And the next verse is all the more surprising, coming as it does after the mention of returning to the dust:

> The earthling gave his *isshah* the name *Chawwah* (Living One), because she was mother of all life.
>
> (Genesis 3:20)

The woman receives a new name, and what a name it is! She is no longer just called *isshah* but *Chawwah* (in English Eve), the Living One. Although the *adam* gives her the new name, it should be remembered that one of his tasks in this story is to collaborate with God in the work of creation by being the name-giver (cf. 2:19-20, 23). The woman's new name should thus be seen as a reflection of her God-given status. Despite what she has done, she has not lost her identity as the "help" that makes it possible for humankind to be what it was called to be by God.

In this verse, the continuing validity of the divine promise and blessing is linked to Eve's status as mother, but we would miss the point entirely were we to reduce her role to one of child-bearing. Giving birth here functions as a visible manifestation of God's fundamental intention to give humanity the fullness of life. This outlook is characteristic of the Bible, where every new birth is welcomed as a new beginning, an indication that God has not forsaken his people. It is as if each time a child comes into the world, God renews concretely his covenant with humanity and life triumphs symbolically over death. A newborn child is a tangible sign, we should almost say a sacrament, of the divine promise of blessing hidden at the heart of creation.

Provisional Acts of Protection

Following the divine verdicts pronounced upon the snake, the woman and the man, the story ends in a somewhat surprising fashion. After fashioning clothes for them, God expels them from the garden to till the soil. This in itself would not be an incomprehensible ending, but God's motives may well leave us somewhat perplexed:

> And the Lord God said, "Look, the earthling has become
> like one of us, knowing right and wrong. And now,
> heaven forbid that he reach out his hand and take from
> the tree of life too and eat of it, and live for ever!"
>
> (Genesis 3:22)

Is God indeed jealous of his creatures? If this is so, then
the snake was right all along and our interpretation of the story
is flawed. We can perhaps begin to understand this passage by
noting that in verses 22-24, there is no longer any mention of
the woman. The unique actor in these verses, besides God, is
ha-adam. And too, there is that curious expression, *one of us*,
which points to the archaic notion of the divine council: in the
narrative itself, there is only one God. These are clues that these
verses retain traces of an older version of the story. Indeed, the
motif of a human being who steals or attempts to steal the divine
gift and is punished for overstepping his bounds is widespread
in the mythology of the region. We are perhaps most familiar
with it from the Prometheus myth of the Greeks. Quite plausibly,
a similar story served as the substratum of Genesis 2–3, but was
extensively reworked by the biblical author to bring it into line
with his theology. The beginning and end of the story could well
have been the parts which were retouched the least.

The question we need to ask then is this: what is the function of this ending in the final version of the story, despite the
lack of a perfect accord? Let us begin by examining the previous
verse, which shows God clothing the couple in garments of skin.
This obviously refers to verse 7, which told how, after eating
the fruit, the man and the woman knew they were naked and
felt the need to hide and protect themselves. By clothing them,
then, God ratifies the new state of affairs, according a provisional
approbation to human culture in a world where humans are no

longer enfolded in divine glory. The supreme realist, God makes use of every means possible to enable his creatures to go forward in the midst of a flawed world, protecting them from fully experiencing the negative consequences of their actions.

If we read the following verses in this light, we can see that they have a similar function in the story as we have it. Sending the earthling out of the garden, in addition to expressing the loss of the original blessing, is to be understood here as an act of protection. Human beings are not yet ready for the fullness of life; to acquire it in their current state would be an unmitigated disaster. Since at this point God's Law does not serve as a "pedagogue" to lead them gradually to life, more drastic measures need to be taken for the time being. To go back to our parable of the children playing in the backyard, the parents, finally realizing that the children are too young to obey their command not to play in the street, decide to build a fence around the yard, to prevent disaster until the little ones are old enough to understand.

This reading of the text requires us to interpret the words *the earthling has become like one of us, knowing good and evil* in a somewhat ironic sense. Now that he has turned away from the authentic Source and made himself into a god, the earthling needs more than ever to be protected from himself. He needs to be sent back to his origins, the *adamah*, in order to rediscover his true identity, to learn humility. Being sent out of the garden can conceivably be described as a "punishment," but if so, it is one whose intention is entirely positive — to make possible new steps forward in the right direction. It is significant that this story has been placed not at the end but at the beginning of the Bible, since the rest of the Bible tells precisely of God's unceasing attempts to lead humanity back to the fullness of life in a communion with him.

The chapter ends with the image of the tree of life guarded by the cherubim and the flaming sword. When we looked at the tree(s) at the center of the garden in the previous chapter, we saw there in embryo the category of the "holy" or "sacred," a part of our world that points beyond itself and that thus needs to be shielded from human manipulation. When the humans were still living in harmony with their Creator in a relationship characterized by trust, the holy place or object was protected solely by the divine command. Now there is the fiery sword. The narrative thus seems to suggest that the sacred fear or awe which we associate with the holy is a later addition motivated by human disobedience. In a world where humans walked hand in hand with God, it seems to say, the dividing-line between the profane and the holy would be much less dramatic, and the notion of fear unnecessary. We are reminded of the words of Saint John: *There is no fear in love, but the fullness of love casts out fear.... Whoever fears is not perfected in love* (1 John 4:18). Although perfection in love is God's deepest wish for his creatures, it is obvious that a centuries-long journey will be necessary for it to become a reality.

An "Original Sin"?

Before bringing this chapter to a close, a few words need to be said about the significance of this story set in its wider context.

Taken by itself, Genesis 2-3 has all the earmarks of a parable attempting to define true wisdom. In story form, it shows that the road to authentic life is found not by simply acting according to our desires or paying attention to our sensations, nor by placing criteria such as technical expertise and efficiency at the center of our decisions, but in discerning and listening to the voice of that Other whom believers call God. We are set before an alternative: on the one hand the determination to follow solely our own urgings and to live in absolute autonomy, which leads in the story to division, frustration and loss of the original blessing both for ourselves and for our world; and on the other the attempt to live in harmony with the Creator, discovering our existence as a call to collaborate with God's work of creation and to nurture and pass on the divine gift of life. The author emphasizes the importance of this teaching by setting it at the "beginning" of history; in this way it describes a fundamental choice that determines the life of every human being who comes into this world.

The story also tells us that even when we make the wrong choices, God does not give up on us, but continually seeks new ways to show us the folly of a self-centered approach to life and to bring us back to a relationship with him. It is thus fundamentally open-ended, notwithstanding the fact that it ends on a pessimistic note.

At one stage, however, this narrative was linked to another creation story and placed at the beginning of the Book of Genesis and therefore of the Bible. This position shifts to a certain extent the emphasis of the text. On the one hand, as has already been mentioned, its anthropological focus balances and completes the vision of Genesis 1, while in its turn it benefits by being associated with the more encompassing and more optimistic vision of the opening chapter.

The other major change is that the historical character of the narrative is reinforced. In its current setting at the beginning of the Bible, it is not only a parable describing a potential choice offered to every human being. It affirms rather that, in a certain sense, this choice has already been made in human history and we are suffering the consequences, whether we like it or not. The place occupied by the text in the Bible calls us to take this historical dimension seriously. In today's world, of course, there are relatively few Jews or Christians who would maintain that Genesis 2-3 tells the story of two historical individuals who actually lived in a garden at a specific time and place. It is not necessary to be a fundamentalist, however, to incorporate the historical dimension into our understanding of the story. We are simply required to recognize that the original human project has been flawed as far back as we can see, and that our own lives are already influenced by this prior state of affairs. In this context the Christian tradition speaks of "original sin," an expression which is practically incomprehensible to a modern sensibility insofar as it seems to imply that, in addition to our own personal faults, we are somehow guilty of something done by another. It must be emphasized that original sin does not refer to a specific act someone committed at one point in time, but in a word "the contradiction between the will of the Creator and man's empirical being"[29] that leads to inauthentic acts.

In fact, the doctrine of original sin does not arise directly from a reading of Genesis 2-3, but from a reflection on this text in the light of Jesus Christ. It is unknown as such in the Jewish tradition. The essential is already found in chapter 5 of Paul's Letter to the Romans. Saint Paul is not concerned in the first place with human sinfulness, but with the universal consequences of the salvation which comes through Christ. For this salvation to

---

[29] Joseph Ratzinger (Pope Benedict XVI), *Daughter Zion* (San Francisco: Ignatius Press, 1983), p. 70. For what follows see pp. 66-71 of this work.

be meaningful one has to be saved from something, and so it is essential to his argument to show that *all have sinned and are lacking God's glory* (Romans 3:23). It is in this context that he reflects on the story of Adam.

It is important to note, however, that Paul was not a fundamentalist. Although for him, as for the majority of Christians and Jews down through the ages, Adam was assuredly a historical being, Adam was also the "founding father" of humanity and thus in some sense each one of us (see p. 42, note 11). Our participation in the fault of Adam occurs through the concrete choices that each of us make in our own life: *insofar as all have sinned*[30] (Romans 5:12b). In this sense it is valid to take Genesis 2-3 as a parable for all times and places. But we must add that the parable works for each of us, and for humanity as a whole, as a retrospective view to explain our human condition, showing it as already burdened by the failure to live with complete trust in God. Its purpose is not, moreover, to cause us to deplore our loss of innocence, but rather to situate the human adventure as working itself out in the space between the grandeur and the misery of our condition (Pascal), between the call to collaborate with God and the temptation to opt for a presumed happiness of our own making. The story of the man and woman in the garden thus serves admirably as an introduction to the biblical epic of a God who unceasingly sets out to find human beings, so that they can become who they truly are in a relationship of love with the Source of their being.

---

[30] Even on purely grammatical grounds, this translation is preferable to the misleading one, current in the past, *in whom all sinned*. See Stanislas Lyonnet, "Le sens de ἐφ' ᾧ en Rom 5, 12 et l'exégèse des Pères grecs," *Études sur l'Épître aux Romains* (Rome: Editrice Pontificio Istituto Biblico, 1990), pp. 185-202.

Questions for Reflection

1. What makes me feel vulnerable? How can I protect myself in a way that does not close off all possibilities of communication and intimacy?

2. Where do I see the "wisdom of the serpent" at work in our world today?

3. "Even if we forget God, God keeps searching for us." What do these words mean to me? Have there been times in my life when I heard God calling out to me, "Where are you?"

4. How can we work against stereotyping and scapegoating others? What enables us to become more aware of those times when we project our own shadows on to the world outside us?

5. "All God can do is love." In what ways can we overcome the caricatures of God that find support in certain negative experiences we have had? Have I ever been able to discern the presence of a loving God at the heart of such experiences?

6. What ways forward can we find when relationships with others become difficult, when work or studies are frustrating?

7. What helps us not to lose hope when our life seems to have taken a wrong turn?

Where Is Your Brother?

Chapter 4 of Genesis begins with a transitional phrase. Eve lives out her vocation as *mother of the living* by giving birth to two sons; she is a source of life not on her own, but with the Lord. She reacts to the birth with a shout of joy that evokes Adam's cry in Genesis 2:23, when the creation of the woman put an end to his loneliness. New life, rejoicing and the burgeoning of language are shown as inseparably linked in this opening verse.

As is typical of the Bible, the names given to Eve's two sons are significant. The name Cain comes from the verb Eve uses to describe the birth: "I have produced, acquired, procreated." Although some Bible scholars view these words of hers as negative, an indication of self-centered pride, since in addition Adam is not mentioned, one can equally well take them as an affirmation that the divine promise has been fulfilled. The name Abel, on the other hand, comes from a word meaning "something evanescent; mist; vanity," a fitting prophecy of his imminent fate. Following the births, the *adam* and his *isshah* disappear from the scene and a new story begins, that of Cain and Abel.

Shepherds and Farmers

The first thing we learn about Cain and Abel is that the former tills the soil, while the latter is a herdsman. It should thus be immediately obvious that the story we are about to read depicts an age much later than "the beginning." It speaks of a time when human society has become so diversified that different forms of livelihood have come into being. The earth is already populated, since there are strangers around who may kill Cain after his crime (v. 14); there is a land called Nod (v. 16); there are marriageable women (v. 17, 19). Now in many times and places, the relationship between those who till the soil and those who tend flocks or, equivalently, between those who are sedentary and those who are nomads or semi-nomads is a permanent source of tension, and so it is not surprising that in all cultures stories arise to express and explain this conflict. We almost certainly have one such story here, which was then taken by the biblical editor and placed after the account of the first human couple in order to give it more universal significance.

In this story, the two social groups are portrayed as two brothers. The Bible thus consciously affirms the unity of the human race, despite and beyond the differences that separate people into different camps. There is then the hope that, united as we are by a common origin, we may one day finally learn to live together on this planet.

Viewed in the context of the Book of Genesis, the story offers us a new kind of duality. In the first three chapters, humanity was divided into male and female, with the couple representing the primary human relationship. The asymmetrical man-woman relationship is fundamental because it represents a basic truth of our existence: by themselves no one has all they need to recapitulate the whole of humanity. The difference between the sexes represents most adequately the theme of the "other" and the consequent need to recognize one's own limitations and to go out of oneself towards that other (cf. Genesis 2:24) in order to make human life possible. The new duality — that of two brothers — poses an entirely different problem. Whether we call it the problem of justice, of competition, or of jealousy, it is a theme running through the entire Book of Genesis, and is always represented by two or more siblings of the same sex.

Put most simply, the question expressed by this new duality is this: if two (or more) human individuals or groups are similar, with identical desires and needs, why should one get something and the other not? And yet in the world in which we live, where resources are limited and people are different, this happens all the time. It happens to individuals, and then we speak of jealousy and rivalry. More importantly, perhaps, it happens on a collective scale, and there the stakes are much higher. How do people deal with situations like these? In a world where the inhabitants are alike and yet unlike, how is it possible to live together? The Book of Genesis turns this question round and round, searching for an answer. After Cain and Abel we meet Isaac and Ishmael, then, at the center of the book, Esau and Jacob, with a subplot involving two sisters, Leah and Rachel, and finally Joseph and his brothers. But it is the story that concerns us now, that of Cain and Abel, that introduces the problem and presents it with the most acuity. That is no doubt why the biblical author has not just treated it as one story of conflict among many, but has placed it at the very beginning of his epic, right after the story of creation and the appearance of the first man and woman.

The Unsettling Divine Logic

Two brothers, then, with different occupations. Both make an offering to the Lord. Here the Bible speaks explicitly for the first time of religion, reduced to its most essential feature. Beings who are not the source of their own existence, but who receive everything from that Other whom we call God, naturally wish to give back to the deity, symbolically, a part of what they have received. This is technically known as a sacrifice or an offering, and religion in its earliest manifestations seems to have been made up of simple or elaborate rites for offering a symbolic gift to the Source of life, whether that Source is conceived of as a single being or as a multiplicity. This basic procedure naturally varied greatly according to the way of conceiving the divine and its relationship with human beings. In Israel, at any rate, offering sacrifices was not an onerous task motivated by fear or guilt, but a joyful recognition of God's goodness to the nation and the wish to express gratefulness for this. This is evident in the songbook used by the nation in its worship, the Book of Psalms:

> I rejoiced when they said to me:
> Let us go up to the house of the Lord!
> What will I give back to the Lord
> for all his bounty to me?
> I will raise the cup of salvation
> and invoke the name of the Lord.
> I will offer thanksgiving-sacrifices
> and invoke the name of the Lord.
> (Psalm 122:1; 116:12-13, 17)

If there was a problem with sacrifices in Israel, it was a different one. Prophetic circles stigmatized worship that did not express the true inner disposition of those who took part, that was performed as a self-sufficient ritual to appease or seduce the deity. The prophets continually expressed their criticisms of a religion that was not one with the basic orientations of life:

> "What do I care about your innumerable sacrifices?" says the Lord. "I am sick of your burnt-offerings of rams and fattened calves. I am not interested in the blood of young bulls, rams, and goats. (…) When you stretch out your hands, I cover my eyes. Go ahead and multiply your prayers; I will not listen! Your hands are full of blood. Wash them! Make them clean! Take your wicked deeds out of my sight! Stop doing evil; learn to do good (…) This people has drawn near to me with their mouth and honored me with their lips, but their heart is far from me. Their worship is a human precept, learnt by rote."
>
> (Isaiah 1:11, 15-16; 29:13)

But we have not yet come that far. Here, we are simply told that both brothers offered the fruit of their labor to the Lord and, surprisingly, the Lord looked (favorably) upon the gift of one and not of the other. This difference, attributed to God, immediately sets up a dramatic tension that will determine all that follows. Why one and not the other? This tension is not only a source of conflict for the two brothers, but it is practically intolerable to the reader. If we require proof of this, we have it in the fact that, from the very beginning, commentators have combed the text for a reason that would justify God's choice. In the New Testament, we already find the following interpretation:

> Cain belonged to the Evil One and murdered his brother. And what did he murder him for? Because his works were evil while his brother did what was right. (1 John 3:12)

For his part Saint Irenaeus, bishop of Lyons in the second century, situates the problem not in "works" but in the inner disposition of the brothers:

> From the beginning God looked at the presents of Abel, because he offered them with simplicity and righteousness; but he did not look at the sacrifice of Cain, because in his heart, with jealousy and malice, he had division against his brother.[31]

Contemporary psychologically influenced interpretations take this line of thinking further.[32] All of them, ancient and modern, have in common the desire to exonerate God from arbitrary behavior. If God is just and all-knowing, they argue, there must be a good reason for his action. To find this reason is consequently to understand the text.

This intention, however praiseworthy, comes up against two major obstacles. First of all, despite all the attempts in that direction, these brief verses are too weak a foundation upon which to build in order to justify any substantial moral or psychological difference between the two brothers. If such a difference were important to the narrator, it is fair to assume that he would have pointed us in the right direction a bit more unambiguously. As it is, there are only two clear differences between Cain and Abel. The first concerns their livelihood and, although it is not

---

[31] *Adversus Haereses*, IV, 18, 3. It should be pointed out, in Irenaeus' favor, that he uses a Greek version of the Bible (the Septuagint), which translates Genesis 4:7 in a way that makes his interpretation more comprehensible. Similarly Saint Augustine, in *The City of God*, XV, 7.

[32] For example Marie Balmary, *Abel ou la traversée d'Eden* (Paris: Grasset, 1999), p. 106ff. The author, a psychoanalyst, affirms that she spent years trying to answer the question of why God chose one and not the other. She finally locates the key difference in the fact that Cain offered the fruits of **the** earth whereas Abel offered the firstlings of **his** flock; Cain's gift was not personal and thus God was right to reject it.

impossible that at one stage of the narrative this difference was seen as the key one, in the final version this does not seem to be the case. The story as it has come down to us does not give us any reason to conclude that shepherds are by nature more pleasing to God than farmers.

The second difference is more noteworthy. Cain is the elder brother and Abel the younger. Going against established practice in the surrounding world, God prefers the lesser to the greater. God shows particular concern for the party that is usually neglected. Here we have come upon something that is obviously a biblical motif. It is found throughout the Book of Genesis, in the stories of Isaac (Genesis 17:18-19), Joseph (Genesis 37:5-11), and later on David (1 Samuel 16:7). It is made most explicit in the story of Esau and Jacob:

> One people will prevail over another
> and the elder (the more numerous)
> will serve the younger (the less).   (Genesis 25:23)

Turning to the Gospels, we find many words and acts of Jesus affirming that *the first will be last* (Mark 10:31) or in some way overturning customary expectations. We need only remember the perplexity of those who toiled throughout the day, in Jesus' parable of the workers, only to find that they were paid the exact same wages as those who arrived on the scene at the eleventh hour (see Matthew 20:1-16). And the Song of Mary, the Magnificat, even turns this into a general "law" describing divine activity throughout history:

> He has pulled down the mighty from their thrones
> and lifted up the lowly;
> He has filled the hungry with good things
> and sent the rich away empty.   (Luke 1:52-53)

Genesis 4, then, apparently offers us the first example of a divine mode of behavior that reverses the ordinary course of things and thus marks a new beginning. For the inspired author, the God of the Bible is not preeminently the one who provides a given social order with the endorsement of heaven but, more characteristically, the one who subverts that order for deeper purposes of his own. In the story of Cain and Abel, this purpose is not yet discernible; God's choice of Abel over Cain is not explained and so the impression of arbitrariness remains. A glance through the Bible as a whole, however, at least enables us to see that this apparent divine arbitrariness is part of an ongoing logic that may have a positive message to communicate.

And this leads to the second motive why attempting to ground the divine choice in the characters or behavior of the two brothers is not particularly helpful to reach a deeper understanding. There is good reason to assume that the arbitrariness is an essential aspect of the story, and by eliminating it by a rational explanation we miss the main point. In so doing we may discover a host of interesting things about human psychology and ethical behavior, but we will have lost what is essential — the signature of God, here as so often, disconcerting and even unsettling.

Why Me?

Two brothers, then, each of whom give back to God part of what they have acquired. According to the omniscient narrator, God accepts the offering of one and rejects that of the other. But how is this known to the actors in the story? Not, presumably, because the brothers have benefited from a direct revelation from

God. More plausibly, they drew their conclusions on the basis of observable consequences. Abel's life was somehow more successful or favored than Cain's, hence the inference: God smiled on him, and not on his brother.

Our story focuses on the disadvantaged elder brother. It therefore gradually becomes clearer that the real question it asks is not "Why did God show partiality?" but rather "How do I respond in the face of an apparent injustice in the makeup of reality?" Defined in this way, the question becomes relevant to all times and places, to non-believers as well as believers. The biblical author is not asking us to put God on trial, either to justify or to criticize his actions, but rather to examine ourselves and to reflect on our own behavior in a universe where things do not always go as we would like.

To bring the force of this question home to us, let us briefly imagine some scenarios whereby Cain's dilemma clothes itself in contemporary garb.

My sister and I are studying for important tests. We both pray to God to help us, and spend the same amount of time with our books. When the day comes, she gets the very questions for which she has prepared, while I am asked things which were not in the sections I spent most of my time studying. She passes with flying colors and I fail.

Again, my brother and I are taking a trip. We leave for the airport in two separate cars. When we reach the toll booths on the highway, we enter separate lines. In fact, my brother's is even a bit longer. He passes through quickly and is on his way, whereas the driver in the car in front of me has forgotten her credit cards and money. By the time the matter is sorted out, I am half an hour late and end up missing the plane.

Two individuals have worked for the same large company

in identical positions for the same amount of time. They both apply for a promotion and a raise in salary. One receives it and the other does not. No explanation is given, and none is immediately obvious to the outside observer.

Two other individuals have purchased the same model car from the same dealer. One turns out to be a "lemon" requiring thousands of dollars of repairs before giving up the ghost in the midst of a holiday trip; the other runs perfectly for twenty years.

The list of examples could be extended indefinitely, but presumably the point is clear. Genesis 4 presents us with a situation which virtually everyone has experienced at one time or another: the "unfairness" of the universe and, more specifically, the ramifications of that for the relationship between individuals and groups. And we should not forget that, for the Bible, everything that happens ultimately goes back to God. In this reading, Cain is not from the outset the paradigm of evil; Cain is each one of us, born as we are into a world we did not create and whose workings at times bewilder and even infuriate us.

Although it is fair to say that everyone has experienced Cain's dilemma, not all of us react in the same way. What is Cain's response to the situation? *Cain became very hot and his face fell* (Genesis 4:5b). In the face of this manifest unfairness, he experiences two spontaneous and in fact somewhat contradictory reactions: his emotions boil over and he withdraws into himself. To "lift up one's face" in the Bible (cf. Numbers 6:26) is to be well-disposed towards the world outside the self, to be in a posture of communication. Here we have the opposite attitude, one of non-communication, of being closed up, while simultaneously being overwhelmed by anger. This combination of energy both released and trapped, however comprehensible in practice, clearly bodes ill for what will follow.

At this point in the story, most of us can still identify with Cain. Rage and self-pity are natural reactions to being unfairly victimized. And no one can claim to have total control over their emotions. Still, it is what we do with them that counts. It is at this point, significantly, that God enters the scene for the first time as an actor. And the mode of his presence is, to say the least, unexpected. Instead of playing a role we normally ascribe to the deity such as judging or giving orders, God is described here as a friend who tries to help Cain by giving him sound advice in his disarray.

Like a good therapist, God begins with a question, one that simply formulates Cain's state of mind and mirrors it back to him: *Why are you very hot, and why has your face fallen?* By putting into words the confused emotions running through Cain, God offers him the possibility of getting a little bit of distance on them. If Cain begins to reflect, he can turn an unthinking reaction into an intentional response. God thus attempts to awaken in Cain the beginnings of an inner freedom, so that events in the outer world do not merely impinge upon him as blind fate.

And in fact, God's next words explicitly tell Cain that he has a choice. He can *act well* or not. God wants Cain to see that the real problem he needs to solve is within himself. Outer circumstances may no longer be subject to his control, but he **can** control the way he deals with them. Here the story provides an initial answer to the question it poses — how to live in a world that does not correspond to our notion of fairness. Waste no time complaining about things you cannot change, God says in effect. There are things you **can** do; you need to discover what they are and then put them into practice.

God thus makes the alternative before Cain more explicit.

If you act well, will you not arise? Despite its apparent unfairness, says God in other words, the universe I have created will ultimately reward the one who keeps on doing good. Surface appearances notwithstanding, creation is not ethically hostile or indifferent. Patience is required, because positive results are not immediately perceptible, but a good God does in fact lie hidden behind all that exists. Believe in me, God tells Cain, and you will come to see the world with different eyes.

The other side of the alternative is expressed in a more enigmatic fashion. As in Genesis 3:16, the two words "desire" and "to master" express a conflict whose outcome is not obvious:

> If you do not act well, sin is crouching at the door hungering for you; it is up to you to master it.
>
> (Genesis 4:7b)

The difference from chapter 3 is that, in this case, sin is the subject of the phrase. It is personified not in the figure of the serpent, but rather as a wild beast lying in wait in the doorway of the heart, looking for the smallest opening in order to leap up, enter and ravage. One never ceases to be amazed at the way these stories, using just a few words and the simplest of images, express the human condition with deadly accuracy and with such depth. Both chapters 3 and 4 of the Book of Genesis tell us that human beings are not fundamentally wicked but that they are vulnerable to the wiles of evil, and therefore need to be on guard so as not to offer an opening to its destructive power. God himself can do nothing directly to prevent this, since he has given human beings the power of choice. God thus appears here as the "helper," the inner voice that tries to get Cain to become aware of the alternative that lies before him, so that he can act humanly rather than be the mere plaything of a seemingly ineluctable fate.

Jealousy or Solidarity

Cain, however, remains deaf to the divine promptings. By choosing not to listen, he has in effect already made his choice. He takes Abel out into the fields and slays him. The horror and the irony of this act are underlined by the use of the expression *Abel his (your) brother* three times in two verses. The crime is all the more reprehensible because it destroys the bonds of a common origin. And is not every murder in some sense fratricide?

It is worth looking more closely at the logic of Cain's act. On the surface, it is neither rational nor just. Abel had nothing to do with his brother's misfortune, which concerned exclusively the relationship between Cain and God. Truly an innocent bystander, Abel's only role in the story is to serve as a foil for Cain, and removing him from the scene will not make Cain any more likely to find acceptance in God's eyes. On another level, though, we are again confronted with the logic of projection (cf. Genesis 3:12-13): instead of accepting personal responsibility, the wrongdoer projects the blame on to another in a futile attempt to deal with it. He then turns the other into a scapegoat, attempting to remove the guilt by eliminating the putative cause outside the self.

In order to understand Cain's act fully, however, we must see still another logic at work here — the logic of jealousy. For the jealous person, what is given to one is inevitably taken away from the other. If Abel receives divine favor, this means that his brother is deprived of it. Jealous people envisage an intangible good like love according to a material model, like a pie cut up into slices. There is only so much love to go around, they think, and so if the other has more then I have less. Despite its absurdity when examined more closely, this logic is omnipresent in our world. The ravages of jealousy spare no one, and already begin in infancy. The story of Cain and Abel thus concerns us all, and the only way out of the dilemma lies in the realization that unlike material goods, spiritual gifts — and especially love — are not diminished but rather increased by sharing. And if I manage to realize that I am loved deeply for who I am, then the seemingly unfair division of material goods loses much of its sting, and more equitable ways of sharing can always be found.

Contrary to what we might expect, Cain's evil deed is not followed immediately by some kind of punishment or negative consequences. Instead, God continues his "therapeutic" attempts to bring some truth and clarity into Cain's mind by his questions. The first one goes straight to the heart of the matter. *Where is Abel your brother?* God's first words to Adam in the previous chapter were *Where are you?* and here too God searches for the missing person. Since all are of infinite value to God, God shows special attention to the most neglected, the "lost sheep" (cf. Luke 15:3ff). God's behavior expresses a logic diametrically opposed to that of jealousy. The one who receives most is not the one who "deserves" it because of what he or she has done to earn it, but rather the neediest. Jesus expresses this divine logic most clearly in the mini-parable of the physician:

> Healthy people do not need a doctor; sick ones do. I have not come to call those who do what is right, but sinners.   (Mark 2:17)

God's question invites Cain to enter into this logic, expressing what we might call the law of solidarity. All of us on this planet, made in God's image, are called to assume responsibility for our fellows, to be concerned for their welfare, since we are all members of the one human family. Cain's answer, however, conveys in chilling fashion his categorical refusal of this fundamental law. *I don't know; am I my brother's keeper?* In other words, am I the one called to watch over my brother, to take care of him? Placed as it is after chapters 2-3, Genesis 4 thus shows in negative fashion a profound truth of the human condition: when the relationship with God is broken, solidarity between human beings is deprived of a firm foundation. This identical truth is expressed positively by Jesus when, asked what the greatest commandment is, he unites love of God and love of one's neighbor (see Mark 12:28ff). A world of solidarity and sharing is only possible, in the final analysis, when we realize that at the heart of existence we can draw from a fountain of goodness offering the fullness of life to all.

The Cry of Spilt Blood

God continues his questioning, showing that he has known all along that something is wrong, and keeps trying to get Cain to realize the enormity of what he has done. It is never too late to reflect, repent and make a new beginning. But Cain for his part shows himself deaf to the divine appeals; in this entire story, in fact, he never allows himself to be touched in that part of his being where a realization of the truth could begin to change his life. In the end, then, Cain does indeed become a portrait of the individual who has fallen prey to evil and who thus expresses by his life a flagrant contradiction: a member of the human family, he incarnates by his entire existence a denial of this belonging, a refusal of all fellowship. One hopes that this extreme example encourages us, the readers, to examine our own behavior and beliefs.

God's next words reveal a deep truth both about the divine and about the structure of the created universe. Its ramifications go so far that we are justified in suspecting that the inspired author himself was unaware of the full significance of what he wrote:

> The voice of your brother's blood is crying out to me
> from the ground.   (Genesis 4:10b)

Blood in the Bible means life (cf. Leviticus 17:10ff) and therefore by right belongs to God, to whom it must return (cf. Deuteronomy 12:27). When it is spilt, one naturally assumes that death has arrived and life is simply lost for good. But no, this innocent blood has a voice; even after death, it calls out to God. And what does it ask for? In a word, for justice, for the wound to be healed by the restoration of right relationships destroyed or perverted by an act of violence. Since we could easily take this for a cry for vengeance, it is important carefully to distinguish the authentic significance of this desire for vindication from its caricature in the self-centered craving for revenge. The voice of innocent blood that is spilt has an essentially positive function. To the extent that it turns into the call for revenge, in other words for merely reversing the terms of the relationship of oppression, then it has lost its innocence and has itself been poisoned by the violence suffered. Oblivious to calls for vengeance, since in him there is no complicity with evil at all, the God of the Bible hears the cry for justice of the persecuted innocent; even after death their life continues to speak out and implore redress for the wrongs suffered. It would not, in fact, be incorrect to say that the cry of the victims of human injustice and oppression is the primary motive-force of salvation history:

> The children of Israel groaned in their bondage, and cried
> out. Their cry for help went up to God from their bond-
> age, and God heard their groaning, and God remembered
> his covenant....   (Exodus 2:23b-24a)

Contrary to appearances, the suffering and death of the innocent is not simply a tragic loss or waste. It is the paradoxical
prelude to the establishment of *new heavens and a new earth...
where justice dwells* (2 Peter 3:13). The cry of the poor brings
God down to earth, so to speak, and ultimately makes a new
beginning possible on the other side of violence and death. This
theme runs through the entire Bible and, for Christians, culminates in the passion, death and resurrection of Jesus the Christ.
With deep perspicacity, a New Testament text, the Letter to the
Hebrews, affirms that the blood of Jesus *speaks better than the
blood of Abel* (Hebrews 12:24). His life, given for us to the point
of torture on a cross, recapitulates all the innocent suffering
throughout history and is at the same time the divine response
to it, ensuring that nothing is lost and that life will infallibly
have the last word.[33]

At this stage of salvation history, however, the positive consequences of the shedding of blood have barely been glimpsed.
Abel's blood indeed cries out to God, with the result that the
blessing attached to the soil is removed for Cain. It is the *adamah*
which absorbs the violence committed against the *adam*.[34] Once
again, far better than many modern writings, and certainly bet-

---

[33] For a fuller treatment of this theme, see Brother John of Taizé, *Reading the Ten
Commandments Anew* (New York: ST PAULS/Alba House, 2004). pp. 72-78.

[34] This insight remains operative in the Torah: the violent shedding of human
blood, manslaughter, pollutes the land (Numbers 35:33). We likewise find an
echo of this sensibility, artfully combined with a touch of Johannine irony, in
the urgency with which the Jewish leaders seek to remove the corpse of Jesus
from the cross before the Passover Sabbath begins (see John 19:31).

ter than most later theology, the biblical author perceives clearly
the organic unity between the human and the natural world.
And this loss of the original blessing of the ground exercises its
negative effects on Cain. He can no longer draw vital energy
from it by cultivating it and, in addition, he is no longer rooted
in it as a place where he belongs and feels secure. Henceforth
he will be a homeless wanderer on earth, shunned by his fellows and unable to settle down. The story thus illustrates the
far-ranging consequences of the destruction of human solidarity:
when trust in God, the Creator of all, disappears, relationships
between human beings become more tenuous, and in the final
analysis the earth is no longer their common home. It is *shalom*
— peace and security — that makes the world a place fit to live
in, and when this God-given blessing vanishes because humans
become gods unto themselves, then the consequences will not
take long to make themselves felt.

Countering the Spiral of Violence

Cain perceives immediately, and with surprising clarity, the
peril of his new status. Like most self-centered individuals, while
remaining oblivious to the fate of his fellow human beings, he
is particularly sensitive to any risks to his own well-being. He
sees at once that a life separated from God and from the support
and protection of others is doomed to death. While this does not
lead him to repent and therefore to seek forgiveness, he does
complain to God while at the same time implicitly projecting
on the deity responsibility for the new state of affairs. There is,
incidentally, a small pun in Cain's words. Verse 13, usually translated as *My punishment is greater than I can bear!* could also be

rendered *My iniquity is too great to be forgiven!* His unconscious seems to be closer to the truth than his everyday mind!

In any event God, never one to return evil for evil, takes pity on Cain and gives him a mark of divine protection. This is not only for Cain himself, but for an even more important reason. In so doing, God puts a stop to what we can call the spiral of violence. Cain is afraid that, as an outlaw, whoever meets him may kill him with impunity. In other words, once the basic accord that regulates human intercourse has been violated, all that remains is "the law of the jungle," and violence can swell to epic proportions. This sad truth has been verified countless times in the course of history — in blood feuds, wars, revolutions and acts of genocide. Lawlessness tends to feed upon itself in an orgy of self-destruction. So here God takes things in hand from the start, protecting the wrongdoer, and others, from the ultimate consequences of his action.

Having made the choice to separate himself from the human community by his act, Cain no longer has anyone to defend him. In biblical terms, the task of standing up for such a person would be undertaken by the *go'el*, the "redeemer," usually their closest relative with some social standing, who takes it upon himself to get that person out of debt, taking his or her side against accusations of wrongdoing, attacks, etc. Amazingly, here it is God himself who becomes Cain's *go'el!* The God of the Bible takes the side of those who have no one to watch over them, and this does not just mean the innocent poor. God even defends the guilty outlaw, not primarily for his own sake, but for the good of the entire human community. The benefits of justice shown even to the undeserving ultimately serve to protect us all.

The end of the chapter and the following one enumerate the descendents of Cain and then of Adam. This genealogy marks the transition between the era of "the beginning" and the world as we know it, in all its complexity and its diversity. And in this ongoing life, both good and evil multiply. In this respect the figure of Lamech is significant, since he carries his ancestor's evil to a higher power: *If Cain is avenged seven times, Lamech is avenged seventy-seven times* (Genesis 4:24). The blessing transmitted by ongoing life does not imply that, with the passage of generations, evil will gradually disappear by a kind of inexorable progress. The seeds sowed by human beings from their earliest choices will continue to grow and bear fruit, both for good and for ill (cf. Matthew 13:24-30). And in this world where both good and evil abound, the biblical author shows how God remains present, always looking for ways to lead human beings to greater life without violating the gift of free choice given to them. If the way chosen by God is slower and seemingly less efficient than we would often prefer, in the long run it is the only viable way forward, since a response of love to love can never be coerced. Otherwise, it would cease to be love. And for God, who is love and can do nothing but love, in the final analysis that is all that matters.

Questions for Reflection

1. What makes people jealous? Is it natural to be jealous?
2. How else could Cain have reacted when God did not look favorably on his offering? What would you have done?
3. Where do we hear the cry of the innocent today? Is the amount of injustice a constant, or is it possible to bring about greater justice in the world? How? Do I know of

people who are attempting to do this? What way forward does Jesus show?

4. Is the spiral of violence inevitable? What can we do to limit it?

5. Why do some people feel like strangers on this earth? What can we do to make our planet a place where everyone feels more at home?

6. What answer does the Book of Genesis propose to the problem of life with others in the stories of Cain and Abel, Esau and Jacob, Leah and Rachel, Joseph and his brothers? Do you see a progression? In what way could Genesis 50: 20 be seen as a summing up of the history of salvation?

A Tale of Two Cities

The creation stories in the Book of Genesis show us how the biblical authors employ the notion of "the beginning" to deepen our understanding of the meaning of the universe and of the human condition as we experience them here and now. By attempting to ascertain what is inherent in creation because of its relationship with God, the Origin of all, they help us also to see what is **not** in harmony with the divine intent in the world as we know it. This act of discernment distinguishes the faith of the Bible from belief in an inexorable fate to which humans must simply submit. On the contrary, perceiving a "gap" between the designs of God and the world as it is — a gap somewhat misleadingly conceptualized by Christians as "original sin" — opens up a space for hope: one day, perhaps, the two will finally coincide. In the Hebrew Scriptures, this hope never vanishes, and it is rooted not in some kind of natural perfectibility through human effort, but in God's own faithfulness.

Here, we come upon the basic dynamics of the Bible. God does not resign himself to the situation of a world not totally in harmony with his designs of justice and peace, but constantly intervenes in order to close the gap and bring *shalom* to the world. At the same time, God refuses to do this by violating the freedom of the human actors. It is thus with infinite patience, one small step after another, that God attempts to lead human beings further towards a reconciliation with the Source of their being, which will inevitably involve as well a reconciliation among themselves.

The book of Genesis expresses this divine intention using the notions of **promise** and **blessing**. In chapter 3, God's judgment following the fault of the first man and woman was already coupled with an implicit promise that all would not end in division and destruction, with a simple return to the dust from which they came. In chapter 12, with the story of Abraham, this promise of greater life, of blessing, becomes more explicit. It is a blessing which in the final analysis will affect *all the families of the earth* (Genesis 12:3). And it does not come about by means of a kind of abstract and general pronouncement by God, but rather in and through the lives of particular human beings. The Book of Genesis follows the promised blessing as it passes from one generation to the next, amidst all the vagaries of human history. It eventually leads to the constitution of a people, Israel, called to be a *kingdom of priests, a holy nation* (Exodus 19:6), in other words a vehicle for the transmission of this promise of life in fullness to the whole human race.

Restoration and Transformation

Below the surface of believers' lives the hope thus remains alive that the universe, and their own lives, will one day coincide fully with God's intentions. Although this hope is rooted in the divine promise and therefore reliable, any attempt to capture it in human words and images is fraught with peril. Here we confront a problem similar to that mentioned at the outset of this book regarding the notion of "the beginning." Whoever looks towards the fulfillment of the universe in God is attempting to describe, using elements taken from the world as we know it, something that is necessarily outside of that world and thus, strictly speaking, unknowable. The "end of history," like the beginning, is a singularity, an event unique of its kind that can never be adequately conceptualized by people who are still situated within the ongoing process of historical time. And yet to be meaningful to us, that event must be placed in some sort of continuity with life as we know it. Something absolutely new would be by the same token absolutely incomprehensible, since there would be nothing in the experience of those confronted with it to offer a basis for comparison.

When the inspired authors of the Hebrew Scriptures turn their attention to the promise of future happiness, their words thus necessarily express both difference from the present and continuity with it. They sometimes begin by evoking negative aspects of our world, and affirm that these are not ultimately compatible with the nature of God and are therefore doomed to disappear when God becomes "all in all." For example war:

> They will beat their swords into plowshares
> and their spears into pruning-knives;
> nation shall not lift up sword against nation,
> and no longer learn to make war. (...)
> For every boot tramping noisily to battle
> and mantle rolled in blood
> will serve as fuel for burning in the fire.
>
> (Isaiah 2:4; 9:4)

Likewise death and mourning:

> On this mountain [God] will destroy
> the veil covering all peoples
> and the shroud spread over all the nations;
> he will destroy death for ever
> and the Lord God will wipe away the tears from all faces.
>   (Isaiah 25:7-8)

Alternatively, the biblical writers may take positive aspects of our existence and amplify them to the extreme. In the age to come, harvests will be particularly abundant:

> See, days are coming, says the Lord,
> when the plower will catch up to the reaper,
> the one who tramples the grapes
> to the one who plants the seed.
> The mountains will drip with sweet wine
> and all the hills turn into juice.   (Amos 9:13)

People will live to a ripe old age, and children will be numerous:

> Thus says the Lord of hosts:
> Old men and women will sit again
> in the squares of Jerusalem,
> each with a staff in their hand
> because of their advanced age.
> And the squares of the city will be filled
> by boys and girls playing there.   (Zechariah 8:4-5)

A reunited Israel will dwell in peace and security in the land promised to its ancestors (see Amos 9:11-15; Hosea 11:11; Isaiah 51:11; Jeremiah 3:18; Ezekiel 11:17; 20:41-42; 28:25, etc.).

Sometimes the longed-for future is described as an act of creation, and this is understandable, because it is envisaged as a time when God will be able to carry on unimpeded the work that had been temporarily interrupted by human waywardness. Believers thus look for God's Spirit to be sent forth once again to transform the earth:

> The Spirit will be poured out upon us from on high
> and the wilderness become a garden
> and the garden be seen as a forest.
> Then justice will settle in the wilderness
> and righteousness dwell in the garden.
> The fruit of righteousness will be peace
> and the result of righteousness rest and security for ever.
> My people will dwell in an abode of peace
> in reliable dwellings and in secure resting-places.
>   (Isaiah 32:15-18)

We should note that here, this "new creation" takes the previous one to another level. The Spirit does not merely bestow material plenty, but also gives birth to *justice* and *peace*.

Continuing along the lines of this correspondence between creation and fulfillment, it is not surprising to find images borrowed from the first chapters of Genesis. The prophet Ezekiel states explicitly that the world to come will be *like a garden of Eden* (Ezekiel 36:35), and Second Isaiah echoes his words:

> For the Lord will comfort Zion,
> he will comfort all her ruins,
> and make all her wilderness like Eden
> and her desert like the Lord's garden.   (Isaiah 51:3)

The most impressive image of this peaceable kingdom, however, is a well-known oracle already quoted in these pages, found in the Book of the prophet Isaiah:

> Wolves will dwell with lambs
> and leopards lie down with kids.
> Calves and young lions will feed together;
> a little child will herd them.
> Cows and bears will graze together;

> their offspring will rest on the same spot.
> Lions will eat straw like cows.
> Infants will play on the cobra's den
> and babies reach out their hands on the serpent's lair.
> No harm, no ruin
> on all my holy mountain,
> for the land will be filled with knowledge of the Lord
> as the waters fill the sea.   (Isaiah 11:6-9)

Eden is restored, and it is no accident that this comes about by means of a human being, a successor to the great King David who receives for this a special anointing with God's Spirit (cf. Isaiah 11:1-2). He will accomplish what the *adam* in Genesis 3 was unable to achieve, namely to fulfill his vocation by ensuring peace and reconciliation for the whole of God's creation.

This far-too-brief consideration of images of the end-time allows us to draw an important conclusion. As in the creation stories dealing with the beginning, the biblical authors basically follow a logic of **extrapolation**: they start with aspects of the world as we know it, and attempt to show what is consonant with God's basic intention and what is a perversion or deformation brought about by the misguided perceptions and decisions of human beings. They are sustained by the conviction that God's truth will prevail in spite of everything, whereas human mistakes will not last. Their portraits of the age to come, far from being empirical descriptions of a reality necessarily beyond our ken,[35] tell us primarily what the universe is, and what we are,

---

[35] This is affirmed particularly in the New Testament. Saint Paul speaks of *what eye has not seen, nor ear heard, and what has not occurred to the human mind: the things that God has prepared for those who love him* (1 Corinthians 2:9). And Saint John: *What we shall be has not yet been manifested* (1 John 3:2). These convictions follow from the biblical vision of God as incomparable and utterly beyond all created realities (see also Exodus 33:23; Isaiah 40:25; 43:10-11; 57: 15; 66:1-2).

in God's eyes. They attempt to focus our gaze on the divine activity that gives meaning and consistency to all that exists, and that more often than not is hidden from our everyday way of looking, concerned as we are to adapt ourselves to the putative reality of a world not fully in harmony with its origins in God. They point to an original innocence, rooted in the divine and thus never completely destroyed despite the manifold attempts of human beings to do so, and therefore ultimately capable of being restored. In short, they show us the universe and our lives as God's ongoing creation.

Cities of Iniquity

The image of an ultimate return to the garden of Eden, while expressing well the hopeful conviction that humankind can never totally eradicate the divine blessing from the world, nonetheless has one important drawback: it seems to reduce to nothing the contribution of human beings to the work of God. A paradigm of restoration, taken in isolation, would eliminate all positive significance from human history, viewing it simply as a long story of infidelity to God's call and progressive alienation between humankind and its Creator. On this reading, the end turns all the dials back to zero, wiping away all that has happened since the beginning and leading to the question of why history was allowed to happen in the first place.

Fortunately, this paradigm is not the only way the Bible confronts the theme of hope and promise. There is another biblical image, richer in content and significance, which offers us a fuller and more balanced vision of human history. That image is the **city**. We will therefore conclude our investigations with an examination of the image of the city in the Bible.

In the Book of Genesis the city is viewed in fundamentally negative terms. This is perhaps not surprising, first of all since we are seeing it through the eyes of a people whose collective memory retained the traces of a nomadic or semi-nomadic past. The first time a city is mentioned in the Bible is in the story of Cain and Abel, where Cain is called *the builder of a city* (Genesis 4:17). Following his crime, Cain is described as the homeless person par excellence, whose ties to the earth and to his fellows were severed as a result of his violent act. It is therefore obvious that the tellers of this story viewed urban life as basically an un-natural phenomenon. Far from being man's true home, the city is implicitly presented as an artificial environment created by human beings to protect themselves in the wake of a transgression which destroyed organic bonds of fellowship. It is intriguing that the founding legend of the city of Rome also mentions two brothers, Romulus and Remus, one of whom slays the other. Is it going too far to suggest that, in the collective unconsciousness of our civilization, there lies buried the memory that the founding of cities betrays a basic infidelity to God and to the earth, that it follows upon a loss of original trust?

This sense of things is made more explicit in the second mention of a city in the Bible. The legend of the tower of Babel (Genesis 11:1-9) presents a story of human excess and divine response in many ways analogous to Genesis 3. In this story, though, the transgression is not seen in terms of eating the fruit of a tree, but rather as the building of a city and a tower to reach the sky, so that the inhabitants can make a name for themselves and remain all together (v. 4). As in the story of the couple in the garden, human beings aspire to be totally in control of their own destiny. And in order to do so they draw upon a certain practical know-how, here concerning the use of bricks and bitumen (v. 3).

Once again, what we have called "the wisdom of the serpent," taken as the principal or exclusive criterion of human behavior, leads to the subversion of right relationships.

God's reaction to this human undertaking is also similar to that in the previous story (compare Genesis 11:6 with 3:22), an irony which appears to evince a certain jealousy. And the divine response likewise corresponds to that found in Genesis 3: a "punishment" carrying within itself the seeds of a new beginning. The lack of communication and the dispersion which follow the confusion of tongues are obviously not desirable in themselves, but they make possible diversity and the settling of the entire earth, the prelude to a new and more encompassing unity.

Babel clearly stands for the city of Babylon, the great metropolis of the ancient world, and its tower evokes the ziggurats, the skyscrapers of the time, the imposing temples built on the plain to simulate the holy mountain where the gods were traditionally encountered. The story thus shows us the city seen by outsiders and interpreted as a particularly flagrant example of human self-aggrandizement. It is a place where humans forget their status as creatures, in other words beings dependent upon God and, fascinated by the works of their hands, come to believe that nothing is impossible for them. They display an arrogance that, for the biblical author, will inevitably lead to their fall. Beyond the sociological reasons for this view of cities, believers are invited to see here an authentically theological vision at work. Outsiders, notably oppressed minorities, are particularly well placed to note the flaws of a given civilization, and the Hebrews of old were no exception to this. They could see that, despite the grandeur of the ancient empires with their imposing constructions, these civilizations were in fact built on sand because they contradicted the true identity of human beings as finding ultimate security in God alone.

A final example of this negative view of cities in Genesis is associated with the name of Sodom, described as a place of violence, rape and debauchery (cf. Genesis 18-19). For the Hebrews, such abominable practices were the expected corollary of human life cut off from its roots in God, and it would consequently seem a fitting end to such cities if they were brought low one day by an earthquake or some other great natural catastrophe (cf. Genesis 19:24-25, 28).

It is no accident, then, that when God wishes to mark a new beginning, he calls someone to leave their city of origin and set out for the unknown in his company. *The Lord said to Abram, "Leave your country, your family and your father's house..."* (Genesis 12:1). The departure of Abraham is the first act of a new stage in human history — an existence in faith, trust in God. At the beginning of the Bible, this means living as pilgrims, sojourners on earth. The wandering life of God's people is clearly contrasted with the sedentary and urban existence of their enemies. Believers are men and women on the road, sustained only by their trust in God, whereas cities are presented as the refuge of those who put their trust in the works of their own hands, attempting to gain full control over the whole of life and its vagaries.

Towards the House of the Lord

This outlook antipathetic to urban civilization continues throughout the Hebrew Scriptures. It finds expression notably in the oracles of the prophets against the surrounding nations and empires that menaced them, often personified in the figure of their rulers. However imposing these world powers may seem to be on the surface, and despite their short-term successes, from the prophets' viewpoint their pride and inflated pretensions will inevitably bring them to a sorry end. Here is Ezekiel, for example, predicting the fate of the city of Tyre, a great commercial and maritime power of his time:

> How did you perish, located on the sea,
> city of renown
> which was mighty on the sea;
> she and her citizens
> who spread terror on all who dwelt there?
> Now the coastlands shudder on the day of your ruin,
> the islands in the sea are terrified at your end.
>
> (Ezekiel 26:17-18)

And the prophet then stigmatizes the ruler of that city in terms that remind us of Adam's fault in Genesis 3:

> Because your heart became proud
> you said, "I am a god;
> I inhabit a divine dwelling
> in the midst of the sea."
> Though you are an earthling and not a god
> you began to consider yourself a god.
> See, you are wiser than Daniel;
> no secret eludes you. (...)
> That is why, thus says the Lord God,
> because you began to consider yourself a god,
> for this reason I will bring foreigners against you,
> the most terrifying of nations.
> They will draw their swords against your fine wisdom;
> they will desecrate your splendor. (...)
> Once you were a model of perfection,

full of wisdom, perfect in beauty
in Eden, the garden of God. (...)
Because of your beauty your heart became proud;
your wisdom was corrupted on account of your splendor.
I have cast you down to the ground,
I made you a show for kings.   (Ezekiel 28:1-17)

By the time the prophet Ezekiel and his counterparts were proclaiming the Word of God, however, the situation had changed significantly. The antitype to the city of iniquity had already been in existence for some time. The great King David, anxious to unify the disparate clans and families who worshipped the God of Israel, sought a place located between the tribes of the North and the South to serve as his capital. He found it in Salem, a Jebusite fortress-city built on Mount Zion; conquered by him, it became the royal residence, Jerusalem. Undoubtedly realizing that so great a departure from traditional practice in Israel would not be easily countenanced by the population, David did something that would have profound repercussions for the faith of the nation: he took the Ark of the Covenant, the symbol of the ancient pilgrim faith of the desert, and brought it to Jerusalem (see 2 Samuel 5-6). His son Solomon in his turn would build the great Temple that housed the Ark and thus became the symbol of religious and political unity for the nation (see 1 Kings 5-9).

The shift in Israel's faith which accompanied the transition to a monarchy certainly did not happen in a day, and not without overcoming serious resistances.[36] In the end, however, believers

---

[36] For a more in-depth examination of the crisis of faith involved when Israel evolved from a loose collection of clans to a well-organized monarchy, see my book *The Pilgrim God: A Biblical Journey* (Pastoral Press/Veritas, 1985, 1990) pp. 56-93.

managed to reconcile old and new. While retaining the best of the old faith in a pilgrim God beyond all human categories and institutions, calling them to a fundamental openness to the unknown, they gave to that faith points of anchorage in the present. The holy city, site of God's house and of the Davidic dynasty, became a tangible expression of a basic truth of biblical faith: when God enters history, this inevitably creates bonds between human beings. Although believers are called to follow a pilgrim God and not settle down on this earth, their faith is not a flight from this-worldly realities into a purely "spiritual" realm; rather, it involves a new way of living together on this earth. Faith inevitably has a "political" dimension (from the Greek word *polis*, "city"); it leads to reconciliation and mutuality starting with all those who root their lives in God.

The significance of Jerusalem is thus to be a place of encounter with God and consequently a sign of unity for the nation. This is clearly expressed in the traditional practice for believers in Israel to make a pilgrimage three times each year to the Lord's city for the high holy days (cf. Exodus 23:14-17; 34:23; Deuteronomy 16:16). Psalm 122, one of the songs sung by pilgrims on the road to Jerusalem, illustrates well the attitude of the faithful towards the city. The song begins in an atmosphere of joy:

> I rejoiced when they said to me:
> Let us go to the house of the Lord.   (Psalm 122:1)

Simply being on the road to the holy city with others (note the plural: *let us go*) allows the pilgrim already to share in the joys of a common life. The travelers finally arrive at their destination, perhaps walking around it first in order to admire its impressive fortifications and its beauty (Psalm 122:2, cf. 48:12-13). This discovery, however, leads them not to glorify human endeavors but rather to call to mind the Lord's unfailing concern for his people:

> ...a reminder for Israel to praise
> the name of the Lord.   (Psalm 122:4b)

These words express in a nutshell the key difference between Jerusalem and the city of iniquity. Whereas the latter is a paragon of human arrogance and self-aggrandizement, for believers the former is a sign, one could almost say a sacrament, of God's active presence at the heart of the world.

This religious function of the city is inseparably linked to its political role. Jerusalem is the place where the *seats of judgment* are found, where God indicates to his people, by means of the Davidic dynasty, the correct way to live together in society (v. 5). In fact, believers kept singing this song for many centuries in the course of which those seats were vacant. They thus continued to proclaim their conviction that faith in the Lord implied receiving God's direction for the conduct of their collective existence. One day, many hoped, the seat of judgment would be occupied once again, and a righteous king would lead God's people along roads of justice to the goal of peace.

Psalm 122 ends with some wordplay on the notion of peace. The hearers are encouraged to ask (*sha'alu*) for peace (*shalom*) and freedom from anxiety, security (*shaliah*) for *Yru-shalam*. Jerusalem is truly called to be the City of *shalom*, where the fullness of life is glimpsed in the harmony among humans living as one family in the house of God. And this revelation to Israel will not fail to have consequences for the entire inhabited world. In the end-time, according to the prophets, all nations will make the pilgrimage to Jerusalem to learn from God how to live, and the result will be peace on earth for all:

It will come to pass in the latter days
that the mountain of the house of the Lord
will be firmly established over all the mountains
and be lifted up above the hills.
All the nations will stream to it
and numerous peoples go up to it and say,
"Come, let us go up to the mountain of the Lord,
to the house of the God of Jacob;
he will teach us his ways
and we will walk in his paths."
For from Zion comes God's teaching (Torah)
and the word of the Lord from Jerusalem.
God will judge between nations
and decide among numerous peoples.
They will beat their swords into plowshares
and their spears into pruning-knives;
nation shall not lift up sword against nation,
and no longer learn the arts of war.
(Isaiah 2:2-4=Micah 4:1-3; cf. Zechariah 8:20-23; 14:16)

Responsibility or Privilege?

The Hebrew Bible thus develops the notion of the city in two opposite directions. At first it appears as a place of iniquity, founded upon human self-aggrandizement in opposition to trust in God. The journey of faith requires a rejection of that city, and calls believers to set out as sojourners in the company of the pilgrim God. Later on, however, the imagination of God's people is captivated by the vision of another city, Jerusalem, where God's presence in the midst of the faithful leads to a new way of being together, a life shared in mutual harmony. Before discovering how this tale of two cities is used to describe the direction and the end of history, however, we need to deepen our understanding of the relationship between these images and the actual historical condition of believers in the world.

In fact, neither of these two cities is simply identical with the empirical places which have given them their name. Although the psalmist could celebrate Jerusalem as the city of peace and the virtual center of the world, already in those days there were believers who had grasped that there was nothing automatic about this. They understood that the nation and its capital would enjoy peace only as long as their inhabitants remained faithful to the covenant with God and attempted to put into practice the divine injunctions to live in justice and solidarity. The exalted status of the city was not a privilege guaranteeing immunity from the problems of life; being a resident of that city conferred the duty to live in a corresponding way. In the biblical revelation, the promise of greater life inevitably involves a responsibility to take the steps necessary for that life to take shape in the concrete circumstances of one's own existence.

In fact, the great prophets of Israel often struggled against a "magical" understanding of the promises to the nation. The prophet Isaiah was the one who expressed this most clearly with respect to the city of Jerusalem. His words are all the more significant since he was a lifelong resident of the capital, deeply attached to the traditions that accorded it a special significance in God's eyes. Yet for Isaiah there was nothing automatic about this, and so he was able to criticize the sins of the capital in no uncertain terms:

> How did she become a whore, the faithful city?
> Once full of justice, where integrity used to dwell,
> and now, murderers!
> Your silver has turned into dross;
> your liquor is cut with water.

> Your officials are rebellious,
> accomplices of robbers,
> all in love with bribes,
> running after presents.
> They do not render justice to the orphan,
> and the widow's case does not come before them.
>
> (Isaiah 1:21-23)

In the ancient world, cities were personified as feminine figures, and so here the faithful bride of yesteryear has now become a prostitute (cf. Hosea 2:4ff). Later prophets continued along these lines in their criticism of Jerusalem, ultimately identified with the nation as a whole (cf. Jeremiah 6:6-7; 7:3-14; 19:1-15; Ezekiel 15; 22-23 etc.). Isaiah for his part remained firmly convinced that God's faithfulness to his unfaithful people would ultimately lead to a restoration of the city, purified and transformed into what it was always meant to be:

> I will turn my hand against you
> and purify your dross with lye.
> I will remove all your impurities.
> I will restore your judges to what they were at first,
> your advisors to what they were in the beginning.
> After that you will be called City-of-Justice,
> Faithful City.
> Zion will be redeemed by judgment,
> and those in her who repent, with righteousness.
>
> (Isaiah 1:25-27)

What is of particular interest to us here is to note that, from a very early time, there were believers in Israel who understood that Jerusalem as God's city was not simply identical with the empirical capital of the nation. They sensed implicitly the complex relationship between the two which followed from the unique character of Israel's God. Certainly, God had chosen this people in order to enter into a special relationship with them, and God would remain faithful to what he had promised. At the same time, the people had no right to appropriate these promises as a personal possession according them an infallible guarantee of salvation. Understood correctly, the faith of Israel excludes any narrowly nationalistic pride; it counteracts a "God on our side" mentality that would use the deity to shore up the claims of one nation or one group against others. Even if the holy city was a "point of crystallization" that expressed God's concrete involvement in the life of human beings, that city was in the final analysis not a material reality but the working out of a divine promise. Thus, according to the prophet Jeremiah, God was even free to allow the city and its temple to be destroyed without calling his identity and power into question (cf. Jeremiah 7:12-15; 19:1-11). In short, Jerusalem as God's city was not first and foremost a place on a map.

The Lord of History

In analogous fashion, the city of iniquity cannot merely be identified with the various political configurations which God's people had to confront in their long pilgrimage through history. This becomes clear from an alternative strand in the biblical revelation — stronger in the New Testament than in the Hebrew Scriptures — witnessing to a de facto acceptance of pagan society. This tendency at first appears to be more a question of pragmatism than of theoretical considerations: since believers had to live under these systems of government, which at times were surprisingly tolerant of their religion, an unconditional attitude of non-acceptance and non-participation in public life was certainly not the most fruitful course of action. This practical motivation, however, cannot in the long run be separated from its theological justifications and consequences. Let us briefly look now at some examples of this other outlook, to see how they correct and deepen the majority view antagonistic to the city of non-believers. This will help us to deepen our understanding of the meaning of the biblical texts which speak of the city in overwhelmingly negative terms and to avoid a black-and-white, ideological vision of concrete political realities.

We can take as our starting-point a motivation which is theological and not pragmatic, namely the prophets' conviction that even the powers most hostile to God and to God's people are ultimately subject to divine control. This conviction is simply a corollary of their belief that the God of the Bible was not merely one tribal or national deity among others but the Creator of all that exists, the Lord of history. Hence Isaiah could call the Assyrian empire, which in his day was inexorably subjugating the entire Middle East, *the rod of [God's] anger* (Isaiah 10:5). He thus implied that God was making use of this world power before tossing it into the dustbin of history. In similar fashion, Jeremiah describes Babylon as a hammer used by God (see Jeremiah 51:20; 50:23). Such a vision of history clearly does not imply a justification of the negative aspects of these empires; it is significant that both prophets announce their imminent destruction on account of their arrogance and cruelty. The prophet of the exile we refer to as Second Isaiah goes a step further along this road. He describes Cyrus, the King of the Persians who allowed Israel to return to its homeland, as the one God loves (Isaiah 48:14); God calls him *my shepherd* (Isaiah 44:28), and even *my anointed* (45:1). The prophet states clearly that this

pagan sovereign does not know the Lord of Israel (45:4-5), and
yet he is convinced that God can make use of him to achieve
his ends.

Biblical faith is thus not ultimately dualistic. Behind the
most wicked individuals and the darkest powers, God, the Creator of the universe, is the one in charge of history. God can
bring good out of evil, and is responsible for whatever is good
in the activity of the actors in history, whether they themselves
intend it or not. In certain situations, then, believers can, and
even should, participate actively in a society based on other
values than their own. We encounter this situation in chapters
27-29 of the Book of Jeremiah. Some prophets are announcing
the destruction of Babylon and the imminent liberation of God's
people. Taking issue with their preaching, Jeremiah tells his
contemporaries that the time of occupation will be long and that
it is useless to try and shorten it. In this spirit, he writes a letter
to the first groups of Jews deported to Babylon, telling them to
settle down in the land of exile for the long haul. And he even
goes so far as to say:

> Be concerned about the welfare of the city to which I
> have deported you; pray to the Lord on its behalf, for on
> its welfare depends your own.   (Jeremiah 29:7)

Once again, this should not be taken to mean that the
prophet has any illusions about the ultimate compatibility of the
Babylonian empire with the designs of God. Its own objectives
remain diametrically opposed to the divine intentions for creation, and therefore eventually it will fall. But it is not necessarily
the duty of those faithful to God to do anything to hasten that
fall, or to remain in a posture of total non-cooperation with the

wider society. It is outward conditions rather than theoretical or ideological considerations that will show how believers should relate to the powers of this world. They need to discern when active resistance is necessary and when the accent should be placed on cooperation, as long as this does not compromise the essentials of their faith.

"Be Subject to Authorities"

If anything, this question is of even greater import in the New Testament, since Christians do not form a nation apart and must therefore inevitably be integrated into a wider political entity. At that time this meant the Roman Empire, which alternated between periods of relative tolerance for the new faith and times when Christians were regarded with suspicion and discriminated against in the public realm, and sometimes even persecuted for their beliefs.[37] Christian leaders of this period generally preached compliance with the demands of the wider society, insofar as that was possible (cf. Romans 12:18). Among other reasons for this, they undoubtedly felt that if followers of Christ were seen to be law-abiding citizens, concerned for the welfare of society, then that would furnish believers with a persuasive argument against the prejudices non-believers might have towards them. Thus Paul's First Letter to Timothy urges the faithful to pray *for kings and for all in positions of authority* (2: 2), and to Titus he writes:

---

[37] The terms of the question change radically in the course of the fourth century, when Christianity shifts from being a persecuted sect to becoming the official religion of the empire. Such a merger of the two cities was undoubtedly never contemplated by New Testament writers.

Remind people to be subject to rulers and authorities,
to be obedient, ready to do every good work....
                                                    (Titus 3:1)

Saint Peter, in his turn, urges his hearers to *submit to every human established authority for the Lord's sake, both the emperor (...) and the governors...* (1 Peter 2:13-14), primarily in order to counter a view of Christians as troublemakers unconcerned with the common good (cf. 2:12, 15; 4:15). He is aware, nonetheless, that followers of Christ may well be prosecuted or imprisoned for their faith (cf. 4:16; 3:15-17). They should be glad about this, in fact, because they are thereby *sharing in the sufferings of Christ* (4:13), who was himself the first one to be persecuted unjustly (cf. 2:21ff; 3:18). In any event, believers are *sojourners and aliens* (2:11) in a civilization which is on its last legs (cf. 4:7). Their basic allegiance is not to this passing world but to Christ, who will soon be manifested in all his glory. Peter can thus combine a certain respect for the institutions of contemporary society with a total lack of illusions concerning the character and ultimate significance of that society: it is not for nothing that, writing ostensibly from Rome, he refers to it as *Babylon* (5:13).

What we have just seen provides us with a key for interpreting what is undoubtedly the most difficult text in this series, one which has caused rivers of ink to flow over the centuries. That text is Romans 13:1-7, in which Paul's support for established authority seems to attain unprecedented levels, going even to the point of asking his hearers to submit to constituted authorities *for the sake of conscience* (13:5), since *whoever resists authority is in opposition to what God has ordered* (13:2). This text has been used by some to justify blind obedience to the state, whereas others have bitterly disputed it and even downplayed it as a non-Pauline interpolation.

A correct understanding of this passage begins with the reminder that Paul, far from being a systematic theologian writing in a proverbial ivory tower, was rather someone whom today we would define as a pastor and a missionary. His recommendations are often strongly influenced by the specific situation of those he is writing to. The letter he addressed to the Christians in Rome dates from the late 50s of the first century, a time when Nero had recently replaced his assassinated father Claudius on the throne. Counseled by wise advisers, the young emperor was at that time undertaking a policy favoring social concord and reform, one that unfortunately was not to last. Moreover, a few years earlier Claudius had exiled all Jews, whether Christians or not, from the capital following some disturbances for which he had held them responsible. In such a context, a wise policy for Christians was to do everything possible to show that they were not seditious but rather respectable members of society.

In addition, Paul's arguments in this passage are not based on specifically Christian grounds but rather on the notion of *pietas*, very important in Antiquity, in other words on giving each category of persons what is owed them. This is defined in verse 7:

> Give everyone their due: revenues to whom they are
> owed; taxes to those who collect taxes; respect to those
> worthy of respect; honor to those deserving honor.
> (Romans 13:7; cf. Matthew 22:21)[38]

---

[38] But then, characteristically, Paul takes a different tack and shifts abruptly to a domain where he feels more at ease, adding a specifically Christian corollary: *Do not owe anyone anything except for the debt of mutual love, because whoever loves another has done everything the Law says* (Romans 13:8).

This being said, we should add that a closer reading of these verses shows that they scarcely go beyond what we have seen elsewhere in the New Testament. Believers are called to submit to duly constituted authority, since in the final analysis this comes from God, to pay their taxes and to do what is right rather than what is wrong. Although the statement that God is the ultimate instance behind all human authorities has unfortunately been used to lend a divine justification to all political actions, no matter how capricious, it should more properly be seen as a corrective of these. In other words, while rulers may believe that they are in charge, in reality they are under God and have no right simply to govern in an arbitrary manner. The validity of this interpretation is clear from the words of Jesus himself to Pilate, when the Roman governor attempted to impress him with his power: *You would have no authority over me were it not given you from above* (John 19:11).

Finally, when Paul states that no one need fear the authorities unless they have done wrong, he seems to be assuming that these authorities are legitimate and well-meaning. From his own experience as well as that of his fellow Christians, he certainly knew that believers could be persecuted unjustly. Perhaps, though, he would consider suffering for one's faith not something to be afraid of but rather a cause for rejoicing (cf. 1 Peter 4:15-16), since the disciple is thereby *sharing in the sufferings of Christ* (Philippians 3:10; cf. 1:21-23, 29; 2:17). When all is said and done, however, it is probably true to say that Paul, who was a Roman citizen and proud of it, had an outlook towards the powers-that-be that was more optimistic than that of some other Christians of his time. It is salutary for us to realize that there was diversity on non-essential issues among Christian leaders already in New Testament times. Despite the different sensibilities, however, the basic teaching they all share is remarkably coherent: the universe is not fundamentally dualistic; God is the source of all power and authority, and in the end this will be made clear; the current organization of society is transitory, marked by sin; Christians are not called to work actively for the overthrow of present social structures — these will fall sooner or later of their own accord — but rather to avoid all compromises that call their faith into question, to focus on their community life while showing their willingness to contribute to the public good. In short, believers are convinced that *the present form of this world is passing away* (1 Corinthians 7:31b) and so strive to attach themselves to what lasts, knowing that *[they] are citizens of heaven, from where [they] are eagerly expecting as savior the Lord Jesus Christ* (Philippians 3:20). To shift to the language of Saint John, they are "in the world" but not "of the world" (cf. John 17:13-18), since their basic allegiance is not to society as it is presently constituted.

Babylon and New Jerusalem

As it evolves, then, the image of the city in the Bible becomes less and less attached to a particular place. Rather, both the "city of iniquity" and the "city of God" tend to become ideal types of social organization, incarnated in human history in a host of different ways. Both cities make their way throughout the entire Bible until this motif culminates in the closing chapters of the final book. It is of the utmost significance that the Christian Bible ends with a tale of two cities, and it is to that final book that we shall now turn.

Understanding the last book of the Bible, the Revelation

of Saint John, is not an easy task, to say the least. It entered the
Christian canon at a relatively late date, which implied that there
were some doubts as to whether it was in fact an authentically
Christian book. This was probably due in large part to its literary
style. It is a type of religious literature known as apocalyptic, con-
taining such things as dreamlike visions, spectacular and violent
images of the end of the age, number symbolism, a profusion
of heavenly beings (angels, among others) and an intentionally
esoteric quality. People unfamiliar with such literature can be
forgiven for being put off or even shocked by reading this work.
It is as if one opened a work of science-fiction imagining it to
be the morning newspaper!

     In fact, the opening verse, and therefore the original title
of the book, is *Revelation of Jesus Christ*, and this tells us what
is really going on behind the unfamiliar style and images. This
genitive can be considered as both objective and subjective
— that is, Jesus is both revealed and revealer. In other words,
the book wishes to tell us who Jesus the Christ is and how he
is manifested in the course of history as the fulfillment of God's
designs, and at the same time to show how the life, death and
resurrection of Jesus discloses the true meaning of the universe
and of our existence. In this work, the revelation occurs not by
telling stories of a historical nature, as in the four Gospels, but
through often enigmatic images and symbols. Upon a closer
reading, it becomes apparent that these apparently exotic images
have almost all been taken from the Bible. It would not be far
off the mark to say that the Book of Revelation is essentially a
long meditation on the Hebrew Scriptures, and their application
to the author's day, in the light of the event of Jesus Christ.

     Although in dating this work we can only go by internal
evidence, it is fair to say that it comes from a historical set-

ting somewhat different from, for example, Paul's Letter to the Romans. In the author's eyes, the principal danger threatening Christians is not to be seen as troublemakers, but to conform too much to the surrounding society, betraying their own faith in the process. The final version of the book is a letter addressed to believers in seven cities in Asia Minor, in all likelihood during the reign of the emperor Domitian at the end of the first century, though it is possible that at least parts of the work go back to the end of Nero's reign. Christians are under intense pressure to conform to the practices of public life and they even experience harassment; a particular bone of contention is the cult of the emperor, especially well-developed in that part of the world. Followers of Christ who refused to offer sacrifices to the emperor would be regarded as unpatriotic and atheistic by the average citizen. They ran the risk of being denounced to the authorities, sometimes due to hostility on the part of certain Jews who did not accept Christ (cf. Revelation 2:9; 3:9), something that could lead to imprisonment, exile and even execution. The author of the book, himself an exile for his faith (cf. 1:9), strongly urges his hearers not to compromise their faith out of cowardice or lack of conviction, but to remain faithful to Christ to the end (cf. 2:26).

In order to spur them on, John shares with his beleaguered contemporaries his visions demonstrating that, despite the ostensible power and grandeur of the Roman Empire, it is not the last word of history. God is still in charge of things, and sooner or later this will become evident to all. The divine plan working itself out in history will ultimately lead to the disintegration of a civilization built on sand and to the establishment of a world in line with God's intentions for creation. Indeed, this process has already reached a climax in the life, death and resurrection of

Jesus Christ. In describing this absolute future, which for him has already begun, John's intentions are not to encourage unhealthy speculation about events still to come, but to help his listeners grasp the true character of history so that they can better live their faith in the present day.

The final chapters of the Book of Revelation are structured as a long comparison between two cities. The parallel is evident from the introductions to each part:

> Then one of the seven angels who had the seven bowls came and spoke to me, saying, "Come, I will show you the judgment of the great Prostitute seated on many waters."   (Revelation 17:1)

> Then one of the seven angels who had the seven bowls filled with the seven last plagues came and spoke to me, saying, "Come, I will show you the Bride, the wife of the Lamb."   (21:9)

A prostitute and a bride: we have already seen how cities were depicted as women in antiquity, and here the identification is quickly made. Regarding the first:

> And on her forehead a name was written, an enigmatic name: "Babylon the Great, mother of prostitutes and of the abominations of the earth."   (17:5)

And in chapter 21 we read:

> And I saw the holy city, New Jerusalem, coming down out of heaven, from God, dressed as a bride adorned for her husband.   (21:2)

For John, all of human history is thus recapitulated in

the appearance of two cities, which he calls Babylon and New Jerusalem — or more precisely in the exaltation of the former followed by its degradation and replacement by the latter. This motif provides him with an extremely concise description of the entire course of salvation history, and it is thus fitting that our Bible comes to an end in this way.[39]

The Mother of Abominations

First of all, there is Babylon. The visionary sees a seductive woman in the desert, sitting on a scarlet beast with seven heads and ten horns; the heads are immediately identified as seven hills and then as seven kings (17:3, 9). In apocalyptic literature, world empires are at times signified by wild beasts, as in the famous vision in chapter 7 of the Book of Daniel. The image is startlingly appropriate, expressing well the combination of brute force and extremely focused but limited intelligence characteristic of political power when it exceeds all measure. Here it doubtlessly evokes the power of Rome, the great empire which, in John's day, was in control of almost the entire inhabited world he knew. The beautiful woman sitting on the beast would thus

---

[39] Saint Augustine deals with the question in a brand-new context in his masterpiece *The City of God*, written after the sack of Rome by Alaric in 410. In that work, Augustine interprets in turn all of human history as a tale of two cities, a theme which fascinates him ("Two loves make two cities: the love of God makes Jerusalem; the love of this world makes Babylon" –*Commentary on Psalm* LXIV, 2). As opposed to the Book of Revelation, however, he emphasizes more strongly how, on earth, "these two cities are entangled and mixed up all together, until the last judgment separates them" (*The City of God* I, 35). The view of the Christian community as offering an implicit criticism of, and alternative to, the wider society and its political structures is unfortunately lost sight of to a great extent in this new setting.

denote the urban civilization based on the military, political and economic might of the Roman Empire and recapitulated in the city of Rome itself.[40]

The beast in chapter 17 recalls a similar animal readers have already met in chapter 13. That other Beast received its power from the giant Dragon who makes war on the Woman in chapter 12. The vision in chapter 12 can be seen as a long meditation on Genesis 3:15 (see p. 94), especially since the Dragon is explicitly identified with *the Serpent of old, called the Devil and Satan, the deceiver of the whole world* (12:9). The author of the Book of Revelation thus views the world empire as under the dominion of evil. We are reminded of the words of the Devil in Luke 4: 6: *The Devil said to him: I will give you all this authority, and the glory of [all the kingdoms of the world], because it has been handed over to me and I give it to whom I wish*, and of Jesus' characterization of Satan as *the ruler of this world* (John 12:31; cf. Luke 10:18). At first glance, we seem to be at the opposite extreme from Paul's view of political authorities as receiving their power from God. That judgment, however, needs to be nuanced. Even for the Apocalypse, God is ultimately behind all

---

[40]   In an earlier work (Brother John of Taizé, *The Way of the Lord: A New Testament Pilgrimage*, Pastoral Press, 1990, p. 195 and n. 6), I mentioned that some have seen in Babylon an ironic reference to the unfaithful city of Jerusalem. Indeed, in the Gospels, the Jewish establishment is shown as profiting from the power of the Roman occupant to put Jesus to death and in that way prostituting itself. And see Revelation 11:8, where the *great city* (17:18) is identified as the place of Jesus' crucifixion. Nonetheless, those John is writing to in Asia Minor toward the end of the first century would certainly have applied this vision not to Jerusalem but to the city of Rome and to the urban civilization it represented, especially since they carried in their purses coins depicting a seated woman who was the goddess Roma. Still, it is not impossible that a vision originally dealing with the former was adapted to evoke the latter in the final version of the book. We have already seen that images of the city in the Bible are not univocal. In any event, there was no other viable candidate for the Beast in John's time but the Roman Empire.

that happens. The God of Jesus Christ is the true *Pantokrator,* the One whose might reigns over all (1:8, 4:8; 11:17; 15:3; 16: 7, 14; 19:6, 15; 21:22) and who allows evil to wreak havoc for a time before bringing about its ultimate defeat by causing it to self-destruct.[41] This outlook recalls that of the prophets of Israel when they show God using the power of Assyria or Babylon for his own ends. Just like all the other New Testament authors, John is not fundamentally a dualist. With deep perspicacity, the last book of the Bible reconciles God's status as Creator and Lord of history with a view of the current political and social situation of the world as in thrall to the power of evil.

Let us now look more closely at the image used to describe the city of iniquity. We are shown a beautiful woman, dressed as a queen, decked out in *purple and scarlet and adorned with gold, gems and pearls* (17:4). But the true identity of this figure does not correspond to her surface attractiveness and appeal. She is a prostitute, in other words her beauty is only skin-deep and does not mirror the state of her soul. On the contrary, it is used for self-centered reasons only to seduce people, to lead them away from the road to authentic life. Does John not provide us here with an incisive comment on the allure of many cultural products, which promise happiness and even bliss, but in fact only deceive those who run after them by offering them counterfeit and ultimately disappointing satisfactions?

The great prostitute is introduced in chapter 17 and, immediately afterwards, her destruction is announced. Chapter 18

---

[41] John employs the expression *it was given* 23 times in his book. This is what is known as a "divine passive," a way of speaking of God without explicitly naming him. See especially the description of the first Beast in 13:5, 7, 14, 15. God "allows" the Beast to reign for a time. Cf. also 17:17, *For God put* (literally: *gave*) *into their hearts to carry out his purpose, to agree to give their authority to the Beast until the words of God were accomplished.*

is a long and extremely well-written lamentation over the fate of the great city, echoing Jeremiah's evocation of the fall of Babylon (Jeremiah 50-51) and Ezekiel's oracles against Tyre (Ezekiel 26-28). She is mourned by all those who benefited from her, *those who shared her immoral and dissipated life* (Revelation 18:9), while the citizens of heaven rejoice (18:20; 19:1ff). A particularly interesting note in this passage is the refrain that this awe-inspiring product of human ingenuity vanishes in *one hour* (18: 10, 17, 19; cf. 18:8). Despite its impressive splendor and might, the city is wiped out in the blink of an eye; it is truly the *house build on sand* mentioned by Jesus in his parable (Matthew 7: 26-27), the colossus with feet of clay in Daniel 2.

In the face of Babylon and its imminent annihilation, how should believers respond? A voice from heaven provides the answer in no uncertain terms:

> Come out, my people, away from her, so that you may have no complicity in her sins and will not share in the calamities that befall her! (18:4)

In fact, these words, which resemble those found in the prophetic parallels to this text (cf. Jeremiah 50:8; 51:6, 45; Isaiah 48:20; 52:11), are not as unambiguous as they seem. Here, the fact that the city of iniquity is not simply equivalent to a particular place on earth becomes extremely significant. John is not advising the Christian community of Rome, or Jerusalem, to emigrate to another location, nor is he telling city-dwellers to flee into the countryside. Since he sees Babylon everywhere, he is in fact proposing what we could call an "inward migration." Believers are being asked to remember that their primary allegiance is to another commonwealth, to the Reign of God, and consequently to detach themselves from the values of a world doomed to destruction. If they cling to what the surrounding society offers, their minds and hearts will become entrapped, and they will go down in the orgy of self-destruction that will ultimately engulf that world. The call to leave Babylon is an insistent reminder to the followers of Christ first and foremost to *seek God's Kingdom and its justice* (cf. Matthew 6:33), in other words to acknowledge the one true God as the Source of their life and cultivate the kinds of human relationships that follow from this recognition. This implies of necessity maintaining a critical distance with respect to the claims of the society and culture in which they find themselves. Once again, the role of believers is to be in the world without being of the world.

The City of Light

After Babylon disappears from the scene, its place is taken, in a renewed heaven and earth (cf. 21:1), by a different city, New Jerusalem. The contrast with the former city is quite explicit. This one does not depend for its survival on the Beast possessing the power of the Dragon, nor is it the work of human hands. Instead, it *comes down out of heaven, from God* (21: 2, 10), source of its identity and its sole security. Its foundation on earth is *the twelve apostles of the Lamb* (21:14) and one finds entry into it through *the twelve tribes of the sons of Israel* (21:12). New Jerusalem is personified not as a whore, but as a bride. Unlike Babylon, this city's beauty is not deceptive. And like her negative counterpart, she attracts the kings and the nations of the earth, who bring their treasures to embellish her; this city is not just for a small group of the elect, but is a place open to all (cf. 21:24-26; 7:9-10).

The Bible thus ends in a sense with another creation story. If beginning and end correspond in this way, that is because all of Scripture points to a dimension beyond the universe and human society as we know them. There are several significant differences, however, between this new creation story and the original one found at the beginning of the Bible. First of all, the *new heaven and new earth* contain no sea (21:1). We should recall that in the Book of Genesis, borrowing a motif widespread in the mythology of that part of the globe, the sea is the place of chaos, from which powers hostile to God periodically arise (cf. Revelation 13:1); it ceaselessly threatens to overstep its bounds and engulf creation. This new world, by contrast, is entirely pacified; there is no longer any danger of an outbreak of destructive violence.

Likewise, the sun does not form part of the restored universe:

> And the city has no need of the sun or the moon to give it light, for the glory of the Lord illuminates it, and its lamp is the Lamb.   (21:23; cf. 22:5; Isaiah 60:19)

In the civilizations of the ancient Near East, the sun and the moon were often seen as divine. Here then, the implicit contestation of the gods of the nations, intimated in Genesis 1, is taken a step further. God illuminates New Jerusalem by means of the Lamb, who thus replaces the *big lamp* and the *little lamp* of Genesis 1:16. Already in Genesis 1, the existence of light and the alternation of day and night were treated separately from the creation of the sun; here, although there is no sun, there is no night either (cf. 21:25; 22:5). Everything in this vision of a universe transfigured and restored is bathed in light. The city exists in a perennial daytime, with God's glory, channeled through Christ, shining upon it. And, since the city itself is built of precious stones, transparent or semi-transparent, it captures the light and becomes in its turn a source of light. If light bears a deep affinity with the mystery of God (see pp. 15-16), then the final vision of the Book of Revelation translates into visible terms Saint Paul's insight that, in the end, God will *be all in all* (1 Corinthians 15:28).

Perhaps the most salient difference between the creation story in the Book of Revelation and the one in Genesis, however, is precisely this: in the midst of the universe made new by God, there stands a city. Human history is thus incorporated into the work of the Creator, as if all the efforts of our race in the course of millennia are not insignificant for God, but rather are taken into account in his designs. It has become a commonplace to say that the Bible begins with a garden and ends with a city, but this is not totally accurate, because in fact the city integrates the garden within it! First of all, employing an image from the reconstructed Temple of Ezekiel that goes back in its turn to the second creation story in Genesis, the vision depicts the river of life arising from the throne of God and of the Lamb and flowing through the city (22:1; cf. Ezekiel 47; Genesis 2:10). In the Book of the prophet Ezekiel, this river causes all kinds of miraculous fruit trees to grow on its banks; the land of promise is thus turned into the garden of God (cf. Ezekiel 47:12; Genesis 2:9).

Revelation 22 quotes this verse with a significant change. Whereas Ezekiel speaks of *every edible tree*, John has *a tree of life* in the singular. This ruins the image — how can one tree be on both sides of the stream? — but the emendation is comprehensible if we realize that, as he often does in this book, the author is telescoping two prophecies into one. On the one hand we have Ezekiel's image of a divine garden reappearing at the end of the age and, on the other, we can read the text as *in the middle of the main street (...) there was the tree of life.* New Jerusalem is thus at one and the same time Eden, with the tree of life in the center (cf. Genesis 2:9). But now, access to this tree is finally accorded by God to those who have remained faithful:

> To the one who is victorious, I shall give to eat from
> the tree of life, which is in the Paradise of God.
>   (2:7; cf. 22:19)

Humankind's exclusion from Eden and the fullness of life was thus not definitive. At the end of a long pilgrimage, which coincides with human history as we know it, the parenthesis is finally closed. The Book of Revelation views the duration of the universe from beginning to end as one immense creation story, the story of a God who brings human persons into being so that he may share his life with them.

On Pilgrimage to the City

We would misjudge the dynamics of Scripture, however, were we to conclude our reflections with a vision of the future. These pages have emphasized the fact that, in the Bible, evocations of an absolute past and future, in other words the creation of the universe and the end of the world, serve primarily to help us better understand the nature and significance of the world around us and of our own existence. Creation is an ongoing reality, and Christians believe that the end has entered our world in the death and resurrection of the Son of God. Just as for the first readers of the Apocalypse of John, then, this "tale of two cities" is meant to help us better understand our place in the society in which we live today.

First of all, we need to recognize that, whether we like it or not, all of us are residents of Babylon. Particularly in an age of globalization, we are all implicated in a world society where competition and conquest are the rule, where the most mind-boggling technological advances and the most sublime cultural creations are seated on the beast of the exploitation of the majority of humankind, for the benefit of a pampered minority, through overt or covert violence. John the visionary may have seen Babylon incarnate in the Roman Empire of his day, but the city of iniquity has outlived that and many another incarnation. Today it is literally too close to us for comfort. It influences our choices, helps set our priorities, lies at the heart of our quest for personal and collective survival at all costs.

But the good news is that, at the heart of this city, there are many who heed the call, *Come out, my people, away from her!* (Revelation 18:4). While still living in Babylon, they know that their true home is God's City; their values are not those of a world bent on self-destruction masked as self-aggrandizement. That other city, New Jerusalem, is still invisible, in the sense that the wider social reality as we know it radically contradicts the values upon which it is based. And yet it is not simply a utopia, a dream for the future. Walking in the footsteps of Christ, many people are attempting to live as its citizens today by making explicit choices, even if that sometimes means being mocked as idealists, rejected as spoilsports or troublemakers, or persecuted as disturbers of the peace. When these people come together and find strength and support in their fellowship, then New Jerusalem becomes visible for an instant on the surface of history. Their common life is an eloquent witness to the truth that, despite appearances, Babylon's victories are short-lived, that what will in fact prevail in the end is that other *well-founded city, designed and built by God* (Hebrews 11:10).

Here we find an approach that may offer us a way to understand better the significance of the Christian community, the Church, in the New Testament. At the beginning, Christians were recognized because they followed a way of life that offered a clear contrast to the surrounding society. They formed communities of women and men from different backgrounds, ethnic groups and social classes, living together as sisters and brothers, as sons and daughters of the One Jesus called *Abba*. The form and the quality of their life in common was a kind of living proof that, inspired by the Spirit of Jesus Christ, human beings could indeed live together in peace and happiness as the family of God. Then, as the centuries passed, for complex reasons, fidelity to doctrine gradually took the place of faithfulness to a way of life: one was Christian because one held the correct ideas about God and performed the corresponding rituals, while living a life in many respects indistinguishable from anyone else. And the resulting conflicts and divisions which arose between those who claimed allegiance to the same God of love belied their words and veiled the true face of that God and his desires for humankind.

Our task is not, however, to criticize those who went before us, but to rediscover for our day the heart of Jesus' message. *The Reign of God is at hand!* (Mark 1:15). In spite of our brokenness and our inevitable compromises, together we can witness to a Presence that offers a real alternative to a world alienated from the Source of its life. As we attempt to be faithful to the Gospel, rooting our lives in God and trying to live in solidarity with all our fellow-seekers, slowly the contours of the city of God take shape before our eyes, right in the midst of our daily life. This discovery renews us in our identity as *sojourners and aliens* on earth (1 Peter 2:11; Hebrews 11:13), on the road towards our true homeland. And then these words suddenly take on new relevance: *God is not ashamed to be called their God; he has prepared a city for them* (Hebrews 11:16).

Questions for Reflection

1. How do I spontaneously imagine my personal future and that of society? In what ways does the Bible correct and deepen my own views?

2. Is it possible to trust in the future? How does faith help in this respect?

3. Why do people build walls around themselves, both individually and collectively? What can we do to break down these walls?

4. Read Romans 12:1-2. What aspects and values of society do we have to leave behind in order to live as followers of Christ?

5. How can we show that we are already citizens of New Jerusalem while still living in the midst of Babylon? What does the call *Come out, my people, away from her!* (Revelation 18:4) mean to me in practice?

6. The Christian Church is called to offer an alternative to the relationships of the wider society based on fear and self-interest. In what way do our Christian communities illustrate that call? How can our own communities, and the Church as a whole, witness more unambiguously to New Jerusalem?